T0324317

"Learned yet entirely accessible, *How the Church Fathers Read the Bible* offers a delightful sketch of the goals and assumptions by which the church fathers read holy Scripture. Outlining the different schools and rich approaches represented among the fathers, Bray encourages us to follow their lead with the sure and certain hope that, in reading the Bible, we will encounter there the sum and substance of the Christian faith, Jesus Christ."

**—Kathryn Greene-McCreight**
affiliate priest, Christ Church, New Haven;
spiritual director, Annand Program, Yale Divinity School

"The church fathers interpreted the Bible in an interesting, fruitful, and complex manner. To read them well, a trusted, knowledgeable guide is helpful, one such as Gerald Bray. His new book on patristic interpretation—*How the Church Fathers Read the Bible: A Short Introduction*—provides a reliable road map for students just beginning their journey with the fathers, and will also be helpful for those more familiar with the terrain of patristic biblical interpretation."

**—Christopher Hall**
author, *Reading Scripture with the Church Fathers*;
associate editor, *Ancient Christian Commentary on Scripture*
(29 volumes)

A Short
Introduction

# HOW the CHURCH FATHERS READ the BIBLE

A Short
Introduction

# HOW the CHURCH FATHERS READ the BIBLE

Gerald Bray

LEXHAM PRESS

COLLECT FOR THE SECOND SUNDAY IN
ADVENT, *BOOK OF COMMON PRAYER* (1549).

Blessed Lord,
who hast caused all holy Scriptures to be written
   for our learning:
Grant that we may in such wise hear them,
read, mark, learn, and inwardly digest them,
that by patience and comfort of thy holy Word,
we may embrace and ever hold fast the blessed hope
   of everlasting life,
which thou hast given us in our Saviour Jesus Christ.
Amen.

# TABLE of CONTENTS

I. What is Patristic Biblical Interpretation?................................ 1

II. The Clash of Worldviews ...........................................53

III. The Four Senses of Interpretation ........................................89

IV. The Search for Consensus .................................... 107

V. Case Studies ........................................................... 135

VI. Seven Theses on How the Church Fathers
Read the Bible ....................................................... 181

General Index...........................................................189
Scripture Index........................................................193

# I

# WHAT IS PATRISTIC BIBLICAL INTERPRETATION?

## THE ORIGIN OF PATRISTIC STUDIES

Patristic biblical interpretation is the study of how the Bible was understood by those ancient Christian writers who are collectively known as the "fathers of the church." That term is nowhere near as old as the men to whom it refers, and it did not come into general use until relatively modern times. The adjective "patristic" was popularized by the German Lutheran scholar Johann Franz Buddeus (1667–1729), though he was not the first to group the early Christian writers together as "fathers."[1] That honor belongs to another German Lutheran scholar, Johannes Gerhard (1582–1637), whose study of them was posthumously published under the title

---

1. J. F. Buddeus, *Isagoge historico-theologica ad theologiam universam* (Leipzig: Thomas Fritsch, 1727).

*Patrologia.*[2] Both men were drawing on an ancient tradition whereby Christians looked back to the postapostolic founders and leaders of their local communities as "fathers," whether they left any written remains or not. Those who did write were accorded the status of "doctors of the church" as early as the fourth century, when Jerome (c. 347–420) wrote brief biographies of the ones known to him (*De viris illustribus*), and it was as doctors that they were generally cited before the seventeenth century. Printed editions of their works began to appear shortly after printing was invented, but it was the Benedictine monks of Saint Maur (France) who produced the first critical editions of them in the seventeenth and eighteenth centuries. Their achievement is known today mainly through reprints published by Jacques-Paul Migne (1800–1875), whose *Patrologiae Cursus Completus,* despite its many inadequacies, remains a standard reference work.[3] Since that time there have been many translations into modern languages, and new critical editions of the original texts are slowly being produced, though the process is still far from complete.

As defined by Gerhard, Buddeus, and the monks of Saint Maur, the fathers were prominent men of unimpeachable orthodoxy whose literary legacy shaped and defended the theological formulations of the four great "ecumenical" councils of antiquity: Nicaea I (325), Constantinople I (381), Ephesus I (431), and Chalcedon (451). To the conciliar decrees should be added the Apostles' Creed and the *Quicunque vult,* or Athanasian Creed, which were not authorized by any church council but which stand in the same tradition. As time went on, the boundaries of who might be counted among the fathers were expanded. Migne included Latin writers up to the

---

2. J. Gerhard, *Patrologia* (Jena: Georg Sengenwald, 1653).

3. There is a Latin series (Series Latina, abbreviated PL) in 221 volumes, published 1844–1865, and a Greek series (Series Graeca, abbreviated PG) in 161 volumes, with parallel Latin translation, published 1857–1866, which goes up to the Council of Florence in 1439.

Fourth Lateran Council in 1215 along with Greek writers of an even later period, but today most scholars limit the time frame considerably and exclude the Middle Ages. There is no universally agreed cutoff date, but even by the most generous modern calculation, the last authors regarded as fathers are Bede (673–735) in the Latin West and John of Damascus (c. 650–750) in the Greek East. At the same time, ancient Christians who wrote in oriental languages such as Coptic (Egypt), Syriac, and Armenian, though they remain much less well known than those who used Latin or Greek, are now often regarded as church fathers too. One of the reasons for this is that a number of Greek patristic writings that have been lost in the original are preserved in one or more of these oriental languages (or in Latin), making it necessary to include them.[4]

It has always been known that the fathers saw themselves as guardians and interpreters of the Bible, and for a thousand years their interpretations, often filtered through collections and extracts from their writings, were regarded as authoritative for the church. The first major break with that tradition came in a series of lectures by Martin Luther (1483–1546) on Galatians, which he delivered in 1519. In those lectures, Luther engaged with the fathers in considerable depth and dissented from their interpretations at many points. His main argument was that they had not properly grasped the apostle Paul's theology, and in particular his doctrine of justification by faith alone. That failure had led to centuries of misunderstanding that obscured the way of salvation and concealed the truth of the gospel.

---

4. A number of fathers were bilingual to a greater or lesser degree, but hardly any wrote in more than one language. Greek was the preferred medium of communication throughout the ancient period, and it is notable that although translations were frequently made from it into Latin or one of the oriental languages, almost nothing originally written in one of them was ever rendered into Greek. Even the great Augustine had to wait 850 years before his works found a Greek translator.

Luther's disagreement with many (though not all) of the fathers' conclusions was matched by a realization among Renaissance scholars that the text of the Bible on which they relied was in many respects faulty.[5] The Bible that everyone in sixteenth-century Western Europe used was Jerome's Latin translation, known as the Vulgate (from the Latin word *vulgata*, "popular"), which, despite its generally high quality, was inadequate for the needs of those who had been influenced by the new approach to ancient sources that characterized the Renaissance. Thanks in large measure to the work of Desiderius Erasmus (c. 1466–1536), there was a renewed interest in the textual study of the New Testament in its original Greek and of the Old Testament in Hebrew, which transformed the way that biblical studies were done. It was difficult (though not impossible) to fault the fathers on their Greek, especially since for many of them it was their mother tongue, but their ignorance of Hebrew was another matter. Hardly any of the fathers had been familiar with that language, and few had appreciated the extent to which Semitic thought patterns underlie the New Testament, which in some places is little more than a translation from Aramaic, the language spoken by Jesus.[6]

Jerome knew that the standard Greek translation of the Old Testament, known as the Septuagint, was faulty, and he insisted on translating the text from the original Hebrew, which he attempted to learn for that purpose.[7] But even he had been forced to rely on three

---

5. Luther was generally favorable to interpreters like Augustine, Jerome, and John Chrysostom, but he did not hesitate to criticize them when he felt that was necessary. In the context of his time, that in itself was revolutionary, since the fathers were generally held up as reliable sources of Christian teaching.

6. Aramaic is closely related to Hebrew and actually confused with it in the New Testament (Acts 21:40) because to outsiders it appeared to be much the same. For a modern parallel, consider Pennsylvania Dutch, which is a dialect of German, not of Dutch (Netherlandish) as we understand it.

7. The name derives from the Latin word *septuaginta*, "seventy" (abbreviated as LXX), because legend has it that it was translated by seventy scholars sent from Jerusalem to

more accurate Greek translations made by Jews in later times (Aquila, Symmachus, and especially Theodotion) and to consult rabbis when difficulties arose. It was therefore easy for the Renaissance scholars to argue that the fathers' interpretations of the Old Testament were questionable on the ground that the text they used was unreliable, and some of them were unsparing in their criticisms. The result was that although the fathers continued to be read for their theological and spiritual insights, the quality of much of their biblical exegesis was increasingly doubted and their commentaries were quietly set aside.

The rise of what we now call the historical-critical method in the eighteenth and nineteenth centuries confirmed this negative assessment and relegated patristic biblical interpretation to the level of premodern, nonscientific guesswork that could be disregarded for practical purposes. Even scholars who specialized in the history of the early church either ignored it or mentioned it mainly to demonstrate how unacceptable it was. In their view, whatever the Bible said, it was seldom what most of the fathers imagined it to be saying, and so the fathers' understanding, fascinating though it sometimes was, was dismissed as quaint and essentially irrelevant to any serious study of the subject.

In recent years this consensus has been challenged by a number of scholars who have wanted to go back behind the rise of historical criticism and reevaluate the methods and conclusions of earlier times. Students of the early church have come to appreciate just how central the Bible was to its concerns, and that, whether we agree with the fathers or not, the interpretive principles that guided them must be taken seriously if we are ever to understand how Christianity

---

Alexandria for the purpose. The Greeks use their own word for "seventy," which is *hebdomēkonta* (abbreviated as O´).

developed. Among this new wave of scholars are several who have sought to recover the methods (and even many of the conclusions) of the fathers. In their opinion, historical criticism has devastated the Christian world and left it defenseless against the forces of secularism, but by going back to the sources and reactivating them for modern use—a process sometimes known by the French word *ressourcement*—there is hope that the spirit that animated the first Christians can reinvigorate their descendants and revive the church today.

Whether, or to what extent, that can be done successfully must remain a matter of debate and will not be known for some time yet. But what is certain is that the biblical interpretation of the early church period has returned to the forefront of academic research and has to be taken seriously, even by those who are inclined to disregard (most of) it. This has the great advantage of making it possible for us to examine it more or less objectively, in a way that would have been more difficult a generation or two ago. The witnesses of past ages are now free to speak to us on their own terms, and we are willing to hear them out, even if any modern appropriation of their legacy is bound to be complex and possibly controversial. Christians have benefited from this new openness to the premodern past, but the motives behind it are often secular and do not necessarily lead to a greater acceptance of the validity of what the fathers had to say. In the words of the late French theologian Charles Kannengiesser (1926–2018), when describing the revival of patristic studies after 1945,

> Instead of being isolated from their secular context for more narrowly theological purposes—too frequently the practice in patristic studies of the past—the founding achievements of men and women in the early church became more and more perceived as exemplifying the social, political, and spiritual

behavior proper to their own time. This changed perspective of Christian origins underlines the shifts currently at work in patristic scholarship. Thus, in becoming more open to secular questions, the basic status of Christian origins found itself profoundly changed, at long last released from the confines of confessional apologetics. The corresponding modifications within the discipline of patristic exegesis reflects an ongoing process of a much broader foundational re-modeling of Christian traditions among theologians and historians of Christian thought.[8]

Kannengiesser's analysis is a fair assessment of patristic studies as they are now pursued in academic circles, but this modern approach is bound to leave Christians dissatisfied. The fathers of the church believed that they were interpreting a revelation from God. That revelation was to be found in the Bible, and the true meaning of the text was to be sought in what it says about God and not in what it tells us about the human writers who recorded his word to them. Since God does not change, what the Bible says about him must be consistent from beginning to end, regardless of the circumstances in which knowledge of him was revealed or the form which that revelation took. From the Christian point of view, modern scholars who think of the Bible as a record of ancient Jewish and Christian beliefs that changed and developed over time miss the point. To the fathers, as to Christian believers today, a common theological thread ties the Bible together and forms the basis for interpreting it. They would have rejected the modern secular view that this theological unity has been superimposed on texts that originally had little if anything in common.

---

8. C. Kannengiesser, *Handbook of Patristic Exegesis*, 2 vols. (Leiden: Brill, 2004), 1:5.

As for the traditional distinction between orthodoxy and heresy, many modern scholars believe that it was largely the impossibility of reconciling these disparate sources that forced the fathers to choose which ones to accept and which to reject, thereby creating divisions that split the church. Their choices may not have been entirely arbitrary, of course, but they were decided by theological, and sometimes even political, criteria, which then became the basis for interpreting the texts themselves. The result was that many of those texts were distorted in order to fit a predetermined pattern. Obviously those who agree with the fathers' theological presuppositions will be more inclined to accept their conclusions (or at least some of them) as valid, and that is what motivates many believing Christians today. Those who do not share that outlook may record the fathers' interpretations for what they were, but will probably reject them as a guide to what we should accept today, either about the Bible or about the God of whom the Bible purports to speak.

Patristic biblical interpretation is therefore not just a form of literary archaeology of interest only to specialists. It is a battleground of ideas, in which the credibility of the Christian tradition is at stake. Retreating into a kind of patristic fundamentalism, in which everything the fathers said and did must be accepted as infallible, is not an option, despite the fact that something like it is occasionally found in the Eastern Orthodox churches.[9] On the other hand, categorical rejection of the patristic tradition can no longer be justified either. One way or another we have to come to terms with it and decide how we should appreciate (and to what extent we can appropriate) it today. But before we can consider that, we must be clear in

---

9. In particular, the Orthodox often regard the Septuagint (LXX) as a divinely inspired translation, which makes them reluctant to engage with interpretations of the text that differ from it, even if they are clearly grounded in the Hebrew originals.

our minds what it is that we are talking about. What do we mean by the Bible? Who exactly were the fathers and what authority do they possess in the history of the church? And finally, what do we classify as interpretation, as opposed to mere quotation or allusion to texts that were broadly familiar to many?

## WHAT IS THE BIBLE?

To understand the mindset of the early Christian church, we must start with its most important single legacy to us—the Bible. For most people today, it seems obvious that the Bible is a book, or perhaps a collection of books, subdivided into two Testaments. The first of these contains the pre-Christian legacy of ancient Israel, and the second is the revelation given to us by Jesus Christ and his disciples. Most Christians own at least one copy of this composite Bible and many have several, often in different translations. A few even read the original texts in Hebrew and Greek, which are readily available in scholarly editions.[10] Dictionaries and commentaries abound and can easily be consulted to explain the meaning of obscure words and passages. It would be an exaggeration to say that every problem of interpretation has been resolved, but modern readers have more resources of scholarship at their disposal and are better placed to handle the remaining difficulties than has ever been true in the past.

It may therefore come as something of a shock to discover that the first Christians did not have Bibles as we understand them and did not think of their sacred writings as a single collection in the way that we do. They faced difficulties that are unknown to us, and unless we understand what they were up against, we shall find it very hard to appreciate the greatness of their achievement. Books were expensive and few people could afford them, and even the ones that

---

10. Some parts of Ezra and Daniel are in Aramaic.

existed often looked nothing like what we would call a book today. The Jews wrote their Scriptures on scrolls, which were awkward to handle and took up a lot of storage space. There were bookstores in the ancient world, but they were few and far between, and it is not clear that the Hebrew Scriptures were ever produced for sale on the open market. The Jerusalem temple had moneychangers, but we never hear anything about a bookstall, and the sacred nature of the writings probably ensured that there were none. Acts 8:27–35 tells us about the Ethiopian eunuch, a court official of his queen, who was reading a scroll of the prophet Isaiah on his way back home from Jerusalem, but we do not know where he got the scroll from. Perhaps it was a gift from the high priest to the Ethiopian queen. We do not even know whether it was in Hebrew or in Greek. All we can say is that it is the only record in the New Testament of a private individual reading a copy of Scripture by himself. The story does not suggest that there was anything particularly unusual about this, so perhaps it was a more common occurrence than we have evidence for, but the high status of the eunuch must make us wonder about that. A man reading a scroll then was probably like a man wearing an expensive Rolex watch today—not an impossibility, but not something you see every day as a matter of course either.

Scrolls came in different shapes and sizes, but none contained the whole of the Old Testament. The eunuch was reading Isaiah, and that may have been all that he had. Synagogues would typically own a collection of scrolls, though how many had a complete set is impossible to say. Jewish boys would learn to read them, even if they were not particularly scholarly. Jesus was brought up on them, even though he was a carpenter's stepson and received no formal theological training. His ability to discuss the meaning of the Hebrew texts was exceptional, but the fact that he had studied them was not. When he went to the synagogue in Nazareth at the beginning of his public ministry, he was allowed to take the Isaiah scroll and knew how to find the passage that he was looking for. Nobody seemed to be surprised by that, though his interpretation of the selected passage was controversial to say the least (Luke 4:16–21)! Later on, when Paul preached the gospel to the Jews of Berea, we are told that "they received the word with all eagerness, examining the Scriptures daily to see if these things were so" (Acts 17:11). The Bereans must have had the Scriptures readily available, but where they were kept, how they were read, and even what language they were written in are questions to which there is no answer.

The existence of many scrolls helps explain why there was no readily available term to describe the sacred writings as a whole. They were usually called the *graphai* in Greek (*scripturae* in Latin), but that word just means "writings" and in theory could refer to anything. Later they came to be called *ta biblia* ("the books"), from which our word "Bible" is derived, but the word is plural in both Greek and Latin, not singular as it is in English and most other modern languages.[11] The idea that there was a single book containing the word of God was simply unknown in ancient times. It must also be remembered that there were different versions of the sacred texts, even when in principle they were identifiable as one. For example, in the time of Jesus the prophecies of Isaiah came in at least three distinct forms— two in Hebrew (preserved in the Dead Sea Scrolls) and one in Greek. We can be fairly sure that Jesus did not use the Greek one when he spoke in Nazareth, but which of the two Hebrew texts he quoted from is unknown, because the passage he cited happens to be the same in both of them. Let us look briefly at the options that were available.

---

11. Even today, although it is possible to use the word *hē Biblos* (singular) in Greek to mean the Bible, any copy of it that you see will be called *Hē Hagia Graphē* ("Holy Writ"), which is how it is usually referred to in church circles.

## *The Hebrew Bible (Old Testament)*

This was the original text, recognized as such by everybody in the ancient world. It was preserved by the Jewish priests and rabbis almost unchanged over many centuries and has come down to us in three distinct parts—the Torah (a word that is usually, if somewhat inaccurately, translated as "law"), the Prophets, and the Writings. The Torah was ascribed to Moses, the great lawgiver of ancient Israel, and was the foundational document of Jewish religion. All theological argument proceeded from it, a pattern that we see both in the ministry of Jesus and in the preaching of his followers, especially the apostle Paul. It can be reasonably assumed that every synagogue had a copy of it, that Jewish boys committed large parts of it to memory, and that it was the first part of the Scriptures to be translated into Greek in the third century BC. It is also the only part of the Hebrew Bible that was accepted by the Samaritans, who broke away from the Jews sometime around 500 BC, so it must have been in existence in more or less its present form by then. But the text of the Samaritan Torah is not identical to the Hebrew one we now use, and modern scholars sometimes use it to correct what they believe are mistakes in the Jewish versions that crept in later on. It is hard to be certain about this, of course, but when the Samaritan Torah agrees with the ancient Greek translation against the generally accepted Hebrew, there is a fair chance that the Hebrew is wrong, and some modern translations (such as the English Standard Version) prefer the Samaritan text for that reason.

In addition to the Torah there are the Prophets, a collection of records and sayings that were accumulated for about a thousand years after the time of Moses. Before 750 BC or so, the prophetic writings are mainly accounts of what prophets like Elijah and Elisha said and did, written by other people who are unknown to us. Beginning around 750 BC, however, the prophets speak for themselves, and their sayings have been preserved in books that bear their names—Isaiah, Jeremiah, and so on—though the exact relationship between these prophets and the books attributed to them remains obscure. We have evidence that the book of Jeremiah was originally composed by the scribe Baruch, who worked with him, and the existence of different editions of it indicate that the prophet's sayings were collected over a fairly long period, but whether, or to what extent, the same can be said for the others is unknown. Most modern scholars hold similar views about the origins of Isaiah, but there is no objective textual evidence to support their reconstructions of the book's prehistory—it is largely guesswork on their part, based on what appear to be different strands of composition in the book, and not on any existing manuscript tradition.[12] Ancient Jews and Christians knew that the book of Jeremiah had a complex history, but they were ignorant as far as the other books were concerned, and so by default they usually took them to be the compositions of the prophets whose names they bore.

Finally, the Hebrew Bible as we now know it contains a number of other Writings, notably the Psalms, which were collectively ascribed to King David, and the wisdom literature (Proverbs, Ecclesiastes, Song of Songs), which was connected to his son Solomon. The exact status of these books in ancient Israel was uncertain, though it appears that by the time of Jesus they were gradually acquiring a collective identity of their own. The Jewish historian Flavius Josephus, who wrote shortly after the fall of Jerusalem in AD 70, recognized the existence of sacred books that were neither Torah nor Prophets, but he did not put them in a third category. Whether, or to what extent, the early church shared his view

---

12. This does not invalidate the conclusions of modern scholarship, but it does help to see them in perspective.

is unclear. The Hebrew Writings are all in the Christian Bible, but they are not sectioned off in the way that they now are in the text. Ruth and Lamentations, for example, which the Jews came to regard as Writings, were attached by Josephus to prophetic books—Ruth was read as an appendix to Judges, and Lamentations to Jeremiah—and Christians have followed the same pattern. Among the Jews the order of the books varied considerably, but the overall collection was fairly standardized by the first century AD, with doubts lingering only over Esther, Ecclesiastes, and the Song of Songs, none of which is quoted in the New Testament.[13]

One little-appreciated problem with the Hebrew Bible as we know it is that it is the product of editorial work carried out by the Masoretes, a group of Jewish scholars whose task it was to preserve the tradition (*masorah*) of the sacred texts. They were at work for several centuries, from about AD 500 to 1000, which means that the text current today was given its final shape after the patristic period came to an end. We therefore cannot expect that the church fathers would have conformed to it. This is particularly important because one of the main contributions made by the Masoretes was the addition of vowels to texts that were written with consonants only. The lack of vowels seems strange to us, but the structure of the Semitic languages is such that the written forms do not need them, and modern Hebrew and Arabic both do without them to a degree that would be impossible with a European language. Even so, there are times when a consonantal text can be vocalized in different ways, making it difficult to determine what the original meaning was. A good example of this is the Hebrew word *h-mth*, which occurs in

---

13. For a recent study of the questions involved and the different lists of sacred books that were produced, see E. L. Gallagher and J. D. Meade, *The Biblical Canon Lists from Early Christianity: Texts and Analysis* (Oxford: Oxford University Press, 2017).

Genesis 47:31 and is read in the Masoretic Text as *ha-miṭṭah* ("the bed"). The sentence is describing the death of Jacob, who laid his head down on the bed and expired. But the Hebrew word could also be vocalized as *ha-matteh* ("the staff"), making the text read that Jacob bowed his head on his staff.[14] That sounds less likely, given the context, but it is what the Greek translators in the third century BC took it to be saying. They translated it as *hē rhabdos* ("the staff"), and that is how the verse was quoted in Hebrews 11:21. This is a minor point without theological significance, but it shows what could—and in this case did—happen. The fathers obviously followed the Greek translation and had scriptural warrant for doing so, even if that reading is questionable on a purely text-critical level.

Whether, or to what extent, the Masoretes may have been influenced by anti-Christian bias in their editing is impossible to say, but given that Christianity was a major threat to their survival in the centuries when they were working, that may have been the case. What is certain is that when we examine the readings of the Old Testament in the fathers and find that they disagree with the Masoretic Text, we cannot automatically assume that the fathers were wrong. It is at least possible that the version they were quoting was acceptable in their own time, even if it did not survive the editing process of later centuries.

## The Greek Old Testament

The Torah was translated into Greek in the reign of King Ptolemy II Philadelphus (r. 285–246 BC), who wanted the wisdom of the Jews to be housed in the famous library that he built in Alexandria, though

14. The double "t" in the transliteration is due to another feature of the Hebrew alphabet, where doubling was indicated by the Masoretes not by repeating the letter but by placing a dot in the middle of it.

the rest of the Old Testament was not completed until some time later and may not have been fully available until the early years of the first century AD. The quality of this Septuagint (LXX) translation is variable, but comparison with the Samaritan and Babylonian Torah traditions, along with the evidence of the Dead Sea Scrolls, shows that differences from the Masoretic Text are by no means always to be regarded as mistakes made by the translators. There are, however, several features of the LXX that are not found in any Hebrew text, and these have to be noted:

1. The books of the Torah have proper titles (Genesis, Exodus, etc.), whereas in Hebrew they are known by their opening word.

2. The Hebrew Prophets are separated into Historical Books (Joshua to 2 Kings) and the Prophets proper (Isaiah to Malachi), which are grouped together as a third category of Writings.

3. There is no separate category of Writings. The wisdom literature is placed in between the Historical Books and the Prophets, and the others writings are placed in one or other of those categories. The books of 1 Chronicles to Esther are regarded as Historical, whereas Daniel is put with the Prophets.

4. Jeremiah is much shorter in the LXX than in the Hebrew, presumably because it represents an older version of the text.

5. Esther and Daniel are much longer in the LXX than in the Hebrew, presumably because of additions made to them sometime after their original composition.

6.  The Psalms are numbered differently, and the LXX has
    an extra one that is not in the Hebrew text:

| Hebrew | Greek |
|--------|-------|
| 1–8 | 1–8 |
| 9–10 | 9 |
| 11–113 | 10–112 |
| 114–115 | 113 |
| 116:1–9 | 114 |
| 116:10–19 | 115 |
| 117–146 | 116–145 |
| 147:1–11 | 146 |
| 147:12–20 | 147 |
| 148–150 | 148–150 |
| – | 151 |

The different numbering of the Psalms is important, because the
fathers all used the Greek system, so that our Psalm 23, for example,
was Psalm 22 to them. Modern editors and translators are inconsistent in the way they handle this discrepancy. Sometimes they follow
the fathers without saying so (standard practice among Catholic and
Orthodox writers), sometimes they put both—for example, either
"Psalm 22 (23)" or "Psalm 23 (22)"—or they adjust to the Hebrew
numbering used in Protestant Bibles and in most modern writing.
Occasionally they are good enough to inform the reader of what they
are doing, but not always, and often the only way of being sure is to
check a reference or quotation against the Bible itself. Another difference to be aware of is that the ascriptions placed at the head of
many individual psalms are often not the same in Greek as they are
in Hebrew—a relatively minor but sometimes disconcerting detail!

But by far the most important difference between the LXX and the Hebrew Bible is the presence in Greek of several extra books. Many of these were originally written in Hebrew and fragments of them are extant, but no complete Hebrew text of any of them survives because the Jews did not receive them into their biblical canon. Where these extra books came from and why they were included in the LXX is unclear. It is probable that most if not all of them were composed later than the books of the Hebrew Bible and that the ones originally written in Greek originated in Alexandria rather than in Palestine, but even that is debated and we can say no more with any degree of certainty.

The inadequacies of the LXX were recognized by the Jews themselves, and further translations appeared in the early Christian centuries. The one by Theodotion was particularly good, and his version of Job quietly supplanted the original LXX text. The importance of these different versions was well understood by Christians. In the early third century Origen (c. 185–254) compiled a famous *Hexapla*, a copy of the Old Testament in six parallel columns, which he wanted to serve as an aid to correct interpretation. In the first column he placed the Hebrew text, and in the second he transliterated it into Greek letters so that people could read it. The last four columns were devoted to the four main Greek translations—the LXX and those done later by Aquila, Symmachus, and Theodotion. The work was never copied out in full, though extracts from it survive, but it was housed in the library at Caesarea Maritima in Palestine, where Jerome consulted it more than 150 years later. It may still have been there as late as 638, when the Arab (Muslim) invaders destroyed the library. But whatever happened to the *Hexapla*, there can be no doubt that the Greek translations were the main source for patristic interpretation and that the fathers were well aware that different versions of the Hebrew original were available, whether they made use of them or not.

The LXX text, presumably including the extra books as well as the longer versions of Esther and Daniel, was widely used in the synagogues of the diaspora (i.e., the Jewish communities outside Palestine) where Greek was the common spoken language, but knowledge of Hebrew may have survived in some places. A man like Paul, who came from the diaspora community in Tarsus but who studied in Jerusalem, was intimately familiar with versions in both Hebrew and Greek, but after the fall of Jerusalem in AD 70 and the destruction of the temple, his kind of biculturalism died out. One result of this was that the Jews gradually retreated back into the Hebrew text, especially as they realized that Christians were using the LXX to defend their interpretation of the Old Testament. We cannot say for sure when the Jewish synagogues stopped using the LXX, but we do know that all surviving copies of it were made by Christians, which suggests that Jews repudiated it at a relatively early stage.

## The Old Testament Apocrypha

By AD 100 the church was using the LXX almost exclusively, presumably with the non-Hebrew books (and parts of books) attached. Did Christians regard these "extra" books as divinely inspired Scripture or not? This is a very hard question to answer, and it still divides the Christian world today. The evidence of the early canon lists shows that many Christians took the Hebrew canon as the standard, but those lists do not explicitly reject the extra books.[15] It was Jerome, who knew that these books were not recognized by the Jews, who insisted that the church should not accept them either—for that reason. His contemporary Augustine (354–430) countered that because the books were in the LXX and because the LXX was

---

15. For the evidence, see Gallagher and Meade, *Biblical Canon Lists*, 70–173.

quoted by Paul and the other apostles in the New Testament, the Greek translation ought to be read by Christians as the word of God. The two men never met, but they exchanged letters on the subject, which have survived, and so we have a firsthand account of the controversy. Jerome grouped the extra books together and called them "Apocrypha," a word that means "hidden," though that is hardly an accurate description of them. Today, most Bibles either do not print the Apocrypha or squeeze it in between the Old and New Testaments, but some Bibles, particularly ones that come from Roman Catholic or Eastern Orthodox publishers, continue to disperse its books throughout the Old Testament as they were in the original LXX.

In favor of Jerome's position, the New Testament writers never quoted the apocryphal books, nor did the early Christians preach or comment on them explicitly, though there are occasional references to some of them here and there. From what we can tell, the church fathers had the Apocrypha available to them but did not make much use of it, which suggests that they did not consider it as inspired by God for use in the church. On the other hand, no church council ever condemned the Apocrypha and in later times Augustine's view was the one most widely accepted. But it was not until the sixteenth-century Reformation that any definite pronouncements about it were made. On April 8, 1546, the Roman Catholic Church officially decreed that the Apocrypha was canonical Scripture, and in reaction to that the various Protestant churches sided with Jerome—quite explicitly in some cases.[16] In that way, a difference of opinion from the early church period was set in stone as one of the things dividing Protestants from Roman Catholics. Modern scholars of all

---

16. For example, Article 6 of the Thirty-nine Articles of the Church of England (1571) mentions Jerome (Hierome) specifically.

persuasions tend to agree that the Hebrew Bible has a superior status and that the Apocrypha is "deuterocanonical"—that is to say, of secondary importance—though it is recognized as a valuable witness to the evolution of Jewish religion in the intertestamental period.

## The Greek New Testament

When we turn to the New Testament, things are somewhat simpler. All twenty-seven of its books were written in Greek before AD 100, and in the course of the following century most of them established themselves as Scripture in the Christian church. Nobody ever made an official decree to that effect, but the books imposed themselves because they were generally regarded as authentic records of the events that lay at the foundation of Christianity. There were some doubts, but most of these were minor and were soon overcome. The book of Hebrews was suspect to many because its author was unknown, although he must have been closely connected to the apostle Paul. Others had reservations about James, 2 Peter, 2 and 3 John, and Jude, but apart from in some churches in the eastern Mediterranean, these books were generally accepted. The book of Revelation was an anomaly. After being received as divinely inspired, doubts about it crept in, particularly in the Eastern churches, and it was pushed into the background there, although its status was never questioned in the West. By the end of the early church period, the New Testament as we know it was all but universal in the Christian world and has remained so, with only very marginal exceptions.[17]

One curiosity is that initially there was some hesitation about the Gospels, mainly because people wondered why there were four of them and not just one. Sometime before AD 150 a Syrian called

---

17. The Syriac-speaking churches of the eastern Mediterranean do not accept 2 Peter, 2 and 3 John, or Jude, and the Ethiopian church adds a few extra books, but that is about all.

Tatian, who was then living in Rome, tried to solve this problem by combining the four into one. His efforts seem to have had some success in Syria, but their main importance for us is that they confirm that the four Gospels we recognize were already accepted as authentic by most people, while other purported "gospels" were not.[18] Around the same time, a preacher called Marcion also appeared in Rome. He rejected not only the Old Testament but also anything in the New that smacked of Judaism. That left him with little more than the Gospel of Luke, which was just about acceptable to him because Luke was not Jewish, but his approach was so radical and so out of tune with the essentially Hebraic nature of Christianity that he never got very far. A Marcionite group seems to have survived for a couple of centuries, but it never made much of an impression and the church as a whole always accepted both Testaments as the word of God.

Having said that, curiosity regarding the origin of the different Gospels was an ongoing feature of early church life. In the second century a man called Papias claimed that Mark's Gospel was the memoir of the apostle Peter as dictated to Mark, and there may be some truth in that. Matthew and John were both regarded as eyewitness accounts, and the former was generally believed to have been the first of the Gospels to have been written, which is why it comes first in the New Testament. Matthean priority, as this theory is called, is occasionally revived today, but most scholars reject it, preferring to regard Mark as the earliest Gospel instead. Commentaries on the Gospels were relatively few in ancient times, especially considering their obvious importance, though allusions to them (and quotations from them) are frequent. The Fourth Gospel played an important role in the Trinitarian and christological controversies of the fourth

---

18. If they had been, Tatian would presumably have thrown them into the mix as well.

and fifth centuries, and John appealed to people like Augustine in a way that the other Evangelists did not. Perhaps the main reason for that was that John achieved the ideal of ancient Greek literature, which was to express profound truths in simple (but unfathomable) language. Along with Homer and Plato, he stands out as one of the greatest Greek writers, and his eminently quotable words echo through the fathers: "In the beginning was the Word, and the Word was with God, and the Word was God." "I am the way, the truth and the life; no one comes to the Father but by me." "It is finished." So simple yet so profound—the classical spirit put to work by the Spirit of God.

## Beyond the Greek World

One of the reasons why the fathers believed that Matthew was the oldest Gospel was the widespread conviction that it had originally been written in Aramaic. There is no evidence for that, and the tradition is now generally rejected, but it does remind us that the Gospels are essentially a translation of some kind. The world of the New Testament was bilingual in Greek and Aramaic, and it was in the latter language that Jesus ministered. We know that Paul used Aramaic when he was in Jerusalem, and it must have been the common language of the church there. But apart from a few words recorded in the Gospels on the lips of Jesus (*abba, talitha cumi*, etc.), this reality is largely hidden from our eyes.

Often this makes little or no difference, but we get occasional glimpses of its importance. For example, when Jesus called Simon the fisherman a "rock," he used the Aramaic word *kepha*, which we know as Cephas and which was translated into Greek as *Petros*—hence "Peter." That Peter was not his usual name is clear from the way that Paul refers to him as Cephas (1 Cor 3:22; Gal 1:18; 2:9–14), reminding us of the Aramaic substratum that lies beneath the surface of the

New Testament, and subtly indicating that Paul spoke to him in that language. Sometimes this may have a theological significance that now escapes us. For example, when Jesus told Peter that he would build his church on the rock of Peter's faith (Matt 16:18), what word did Jesus use for "church"? Obviously, Matthew (or whoever wrote the Gospel) thought that "church" (*ekklēsia*) was the right way to translate what Jesus said, but "church" is such a loaded theological term that we would dearly like to know what the actual word was.

Questions like these fascinate us, but it has to be said that they seldom bothered the church fathers. They knew that the Greek of the New Testament was largely a translation, but they almost never made any serious effort to go back behind it to the "original" Hebrew or Aramaic. In fact, they showed little interest in other languages at all. Greek was the universal *lingua franca* and people were expected to know it, or to learn it if they did not. An exception of sorts was made for Latin, which was the official language of the Roman Empire, but that was about it. On one of his missionary journeys Paul encountered people who spoke only Lycaonian, but neither he nor anybody else made any effort to translate their message into it (Acts 14:11). Only much later were languages like Coptic (in Egypt), Syriac (a version of Aramaic), and Armenian used as theological media, and even then it was at least sometimes because the people who spoke those languages were out of line with the orthodoxy of the Greek-speaking church. Occasionally this has worked to our advantage, because books that were condemned as heretical in the Greek world were translated into one of these oriental languages and have survived, giving us a fuller picture of what was going on. But that was not the intention of the translators, nor is there any sign that works originally written in one of those "barbarian" tongues, however orthodox they may have been, were ever translated into Greek. Traffic was all one way—from Greek to a local language, but not the other way round.

In the West, Latin was even more dominant than Greek was in the East. No translations were ever made into the local languages of Spain, Gaul, or Britain, and nobody wrote in them either.[19] After about AD 250, when Greek died out in the Roman church, Latin was the language of writing and also of public worship, which it remained until the Reformation, by which time it was no longer spoken by anyone. But even after Latin became the main language of the Western church, the books of the Bible were only partially and unofficially translated into it. Modern scholars speak of the Old Latin (*Vetus Latina*) version, but this is an academic construct. In reality, the Latin fathers either made their own translations from Greek as they went along or used what others had done. By the late fourth century there were several competing translations, none of which was comprehensive. It was to rectify this situation that Pope Damasus I (r. 366–384) asked Jerome to prepare an authoritative version, which he completed around the year 400. Before long, this Vulgate, as it was called, became the standard text of the Bible in Western Europe and remained so for over a thousand years. It was not perfect, of course, but given the conditions in which Jerome was forced to work, it was well done. It was used without question by the later Latin fathers and remains a remarkable monument to the quality of patristic biblical interpretation.

The ancient world was much more culturally diverse than we often imagine, but in literary terms it was essentially bilingual—Latin and Greek—and would remain so for centuries. But even at the highest level, Christian bilingualism was one-sided. Latin speakers would translate Greek works, but not the other way round, and after the fall of the Roman Empire in the West, even that began

---

19. Eventually there was some writing in Old Irish and in Old English, but that only began after the fall of the Roman Empire, and those languages never succeeded in displacing Latin.

to die out. Writers almost never used both, and by the end of the patristic period it would be fair to say that the theological outlook of a given individual would be shaped to a significant extent by the language he wrote in, as the two halves of the old empire became increasingly estranged.

### The Format of the Bible

In addition to the content of the Christian Bible, we have to consider the physical form that it took. Initially, Christians used scrolls in the same way that Jews did, but this was soon felt to be inconvenient. Before long, Christians were writing their texts on sheets of papyrus, which they then bound together in a primitive version of the modern book. This is what we call the *codex* (plural: *codices*), and it soon became the standard for all Christian literature.[20] The great Bibles that have come down to us from the ancient world are codices—the Codex Alexandrinus, the Codex Sinaiticus, and the Codex Vaticanus being the most outstanding examples. The codex format made it much easier for a preacher to pack a Bible (or portion of a Bible) in his saddlebag, and it was also cheaper than a scroll, though too much should not be made of that. Most Christians still found it impossible to purchase their own copies and had to rely on their local churches, which would most probably have a collection of them. Even so, it was somewhat hit or miss what they actually possessed, as surviving codices remind us. Many of them are incomplete, and some contain books such as the Shepherd of Hermas that are not part of the New Testament. There was no common standard of production, no rule to determine what should be included (or in what order), and—of course—no copyright either. Any combination was

---

20. It may be noted that in Romansh (spoken in parts of Switzerland) the word for "book" is still *cudesch*.

possible, and the wonder is that the texts that we have are as uniform as they are. For all its shortcomings, the church was more careful than many modern scholars give it credit for when it came to safeguarding the integrity of its sacred texts.

One final thing that needs to be said is that in ancient times the Scriptures were not divided into chapter and verse in the way they are today. Chapters were first introduced in Paris about the year 1200 and verses appeared only about 1550, when they were invented by Theodore Beza for reference purposes. To make matters even more difficult, the words were run together without a space between them, and scribes would go on to the next line even if they were in the middle of a word. There was also no distinction between capital and small letters—only "uncials" (which we call capitals) were used before the ninth century—so that there is no way of telling whether Jesus meant "spirit" or "Spirit" when he told the woman at the well that true worshipers must worship God in that way (John 4:24). Modern editors and translators are forced to choose, but the scribes of the early church were spared the need to do so, and so either interpretation could be defended with equal sincerity and passion.

Strange though it may seem to us, although what we call the Bible existed in the early church and its contents were highly revered, in practice the text was rare and often inaccessible to most people. Even great men like Augustine probably did not possess a complete set of codices, at least not personally. Their Bibles would most likely have belonged to the church in which they ministered and come in several volumes exhibiting variable standards of copying. We should not be surprised that people sometimes misread them and produced wrong interpretations as a result—the wonder is that such mistakes happened as seldom as they did.

## WHO WERE THE CHURCH FATHERS?

To those who first developed the discipline of patristic studies, the fathers of the church were the men who had established its doctrine and set it on the course of theological orthodoxy that has remained the gold standard of Christian belief ever since. Their insistence on theological orthodoxy was logical, because those who deviated from it could hardly be recognized as the founders of the orthodox tradition. In most cases there was no real problem with this. People like Irenaeus, Cyprian, Athanasius, Augustine, and Jerome, along with a host of others, were universally accepted as exponents of sound doctrine. They were not infallible and they sometimes disagreed with one another, but on the essentials of the Christian faith they were united. Their interpretation of particular biblical texts might be called into question, but if so, it was usually because they had read correct doctrine out of texts that did not support it. For example, Augustine read the parable of the good Samaritan as a picture of Jesus who rescues the sinner (the man robbed on the road to Jericho) by placing his sins on the cross (the Samaritan's donkey) and taking him to the church (the inn) where he would be healed.[21] It is certainly possible to understand the gospel of salvation in that way, but to read it out of the parable is mistaken—that is not what it is about. This did not matter too much though, because as long as the doctrine was correct (or at least justifiable), the somewhat fanciful reading of the biblical text could be overlooked.

The fathers were honored for their teaching, not for their method(s) of interpreting the Bible, even if ultimately the two things could not be kept separate. It was only because the gospel was clearly taught in other texts that Augustine was able to apply the message

---

21. Augustine of Hippo, *Questions on the Gospels* 2.19. It should be said that Augustine was developing a line of thought already present in Irenaeus and Origen, among others.

to the parable, following the principle (still accepted today) that the clearer parts of Scripture must be used to interpret its more difficult or obscure parts. Parables were not historical accounts but fictional stories told to illustrate a particular point, and if Augustine thought that the point was salvation, then reading it like that made perfect sense.

For centuries it was assumed that unorthodox writers were necessarily wrong, and their works were either not copied or else burnt. Most of what we know about them now comes from their enemies, who often quoted substantial extracts from their writings in order to refute them. Sometimes these extracts dealt with biblical interpretation, as, for example, the Arian reading of Proverbs 8:22, which in the LXX version reads: "He created me, the beginning of his ways, for his works." This was interpreted to mean that God the Father created the Son at the beginning, and then used him to create everything else, as it says in John 1:3. Both the orthodox and the Arians whom they condemned as heretics read the text in this way, but they interpreted it differently.[22] For the Arians it meant that the Son was himself a creature, but for the orthodox it was understood to be saying that the Son was the first principle of the creation, and therefore not part of it himself. In fact, as we now know, the verse is not about the Son at all but about the divine wisdom. Insofar as wisdom is not a thing or a "creature," this supports the orthodox doctrine, but no modern exegete or theologian would base that doctrine on this verse. From our point of view, both the orthodox and the Arians were mistaken in their interpretation of the text, even if we still endorse the orthodox belief and reject the Arian one for other reasons.

The question becomes more complicated when we realize that some early Christian writers were regarded as perfectly orthodox in

---

22. Arians were those who followed Arius (256–336), a presbyter of Alexandria who was condemned for heresy in 318.

their own lifetimes but were condemned as heretics after their deaths—
in some cases, long afterward. The classic example of this is Origen,
who died in 254 but was not condemned until 553, almost three centuries later. By that time his writings had influenced generations of
people who were impeccably orthodox. Should they be condemned
as well? Could a heretic inspire an orthodox writer, even if it was clear
that the latter had borrowed from the former, not knowing that he was
a heretic? That was obviously too much to expect, and the result was
that some writings by heretics were preserved if it could be shown
that the writings did not contain anything heretical. A classic example of this was Pelagius (c. 354–420), who was condemned for heresy
during his lifetime but whose biblical commentaries were considered
to be free of error. In theory, they should have been burned because of
their author, but in fact they were preserved by being recycled under
the names of Jerome and Cassiodorus, both of whom were considered to be fully orthodox. It was not until 1859 that the true author
of these commentaries was discovered, by which time they had been
regarded as part of the orthodox canon of interpretation for centuries.

As time went on, cases of this kind multiplied. There are any
number of sermons and other writings attributed to men like
Augustine and John Chrysostom (c. 344–407) that we now know to
be spurious, but we have no idea who wrote them. Were they heretics
whose identity has been concealed? Nobody knows. The most famous
case of this is that of an anonymous Roman who wrote an excellent
commentary on the Pauline Epistles sometime around the year 370.
It was preserved among the works of Ambrose of Milan, but it was
apparent to Erasmus that this was not correct. The author's writings
were detached from the works of Ambrose, and in the seventeenth
century he was somewhat jokingly rebranded as "Ambrosiaster," the
name by which he is known today. But who Ambrosiaster was and

what his personal beliefs were cannot now be determined. There is no indication from his commentary that he was a heretic, but that is also true of Pelagius, so who knows? We just assume that he was orthodox for want of any evidence to the contrary, but can we say that he was a father of the church when we do not know who he was? That is somewhat problematic!

Somewhere in between the orthodox and the heretics were the schismatics. These were people who broke with the institutional church for various reasons but who remained essentially orthodox in their faith. The first one we have to consider is Tertullian of Carthage (c. 155–225), who is widely believed to have left the church sometime around 207 and joined the Montanist sect.[23] The Montanists were not heretics in the doctrinal sense of the term, but they subscribed to millenarian prophecies and pronounced judgment on what they saw as the corrupt church of their time. Whether Tertullian really was a Montanist is a matter of dispute, but one thing is certain. His voluminous writings were not destroyed or even condemned, and he was greatly respected by later generations, including Jerome, who went out of his way to exonerate him and to blame the clergy of the time for the unfortunate schism that resulted. Another schismatic who escaped censure was Tyconius (c. 330–390), a Donatist who was at odds with the church because of its apparent compromises with the ungodly "world," but whose theology was orthodox.[24] Augustine, who did not hesitate to write at length against the errors of Donatism, had no problem in accepting Tyconius's methods of biblical interpretation. Not only that, but

---

23. Montanus was a self-proclaimed prophet who gathered a following in Asia Minor sometime after AD 150.

24. Donatism was named after Donatus, one of its early leaders. It was a puristic movement in North Africa that denounced the compact between the state and the church that legalized Christianity in 313.

he did not make any attempt to conceal his source, which shows us that, in this case at least, he did not regard schism as anything like as serious as heresy.

Partly because of these difficulties of classification, modern scholars of all persuasions have generally widened (or abandoned) the concept of church fathers in order to include every major writer of the early church period, whether orthodox or not. For secular scholars, the concepts of orthodoxy and heresy indicate an unwelcome theological bias, but to discount such labels is to ignore the very real feeling in the early church that heresy was a reality that had to be combated. It may be that in the fourth and fifth centuries the differences between some orthodox and some heretics were quite subtle, but they were still strongly felt. It is simply not true to say, as some scholars have done, that the orthodox were just one group among many that happened to have the power and influence they needed to secure their position against all the others. On the contrary, there were times when the orthodox were an embattled minority that had to fight to maintain the purity of the gospel. Some people may dispute whether they were right in what they said, but that they said it, and said it without compromise, must be admitted and taken into account. Patristic biblical interpretation was not the exclusive preserve of undoubtedly orthodox writers, but those who engaged in it were looking for the truth and wanted to be orthodox, whether they succeeded in that aim or not.[25]

## The Second Century

It is generally agreed today that the early church period begins with the postapostolic generation, which means that it does not include the New Testament. This makes sense, because after the apostles died

---

25. Kannengiesser's *Handbook of Patristic Exegesis* has a comprehensive description of all the early Christian writers who contributed to biblical studies, subdivided according to period and language.

their successors did not claim the same authority. Modern scholars have sometimes thought that some of the New Testament books were written two or three generations after the death of the last apostle, but this was not the view taken in the early church. Even in cases where the authorship of a New Testament book was unknown or disputed, it was always assumed that it was inspired by God and came from the apostolic age, since otherwise it would have been rejected. The patristic era began after the New Testament was complete, even if not all of its books were universally recognized as canonical. For the first hundred years it consisted mainly of works written in Greek that were designed to promote the truth of the Christian faith in a world that either was ignorant of it or denied it. The key point is that none of these later writings was believed to be divinely inspired or to form part of the New Testament. The first fathers stood on a lower plane than the apostles, and everyone knew it. Their task was to interpret what the prophets and apostles had said, not to add to it, even when the epistolary form that their writings took often bore a striking resemblance to the letters of Paul, Peter, and John.

For most of the second Christian century the church's writers were preoccupied with establishing the authority of the Bible in opposition to Jews, pagans, and would-be Christians who wanted to create a syncretistic kind of Christianity that combined Greek philosophy, mysticism, and the Hebrew Scriptures in a series of patterns that modern research has lumped together as Gnosticism. In the process, they also had to work out what role should be given to the surviving apostolic writings, which they came to accept as divinely inspired Scripture. It was in this period that the New Testament as we know it came into being, even if the precise limits of its canon had not yet been decided.

The writings of this postapostolic era are not "biblical interpretation" in the later sense of the term, but they laid the foundations on which that biblical interpretation would be built by defining what Christianity was, over against Judaism, Greek philosophies, and the various kinds of Gnosticism. They were evangelists or, as they are usually called, apologists for their faith more than skilled exegetes of Scripture, but they made full use of the Bible in their defense, concentrating less on the details of particular verses and more on what we would now call the worldview that the divine revelation conveyed.

One of the most important of these apologists was Justin Martyr (c. 100–165), a Greek speaker who was born and brought up in Samaria. His surviving works divide neatly into a *Dialogue with Trypho* and two *Apologies* to the Greco-Roman elite, giving us a clear picture of how one man approached these very different rivals. Trypho may be identified with Tarphon, a rabbi who is mentioned in the Mishnah, and it is possible that a real dialogue took place between the two men, probably in Ephesus.[26] Justin's argument consisted of three main points:

1. The law of Moses was temporary and had been superseded by the gospel.

2. Christ is God in human flesh.

3. Christians are the new Israel and the true chosen people of God.

Justin argued each of these points on the basis of Old Testament prophecy, continuing the tradition already established in the New Testament itself. In contrast to this, his *Apologies* say little about the Bible but argue on the basis of Roman law that the accusations made against Christians are without foundation. When comparing Christianity to

---

26. Eusebius of Caesarea, *Ecclesiastical History* 4.18.6.

paganism, Justin claimed that the demons who inspired pagan worship practices borrowed from the Old Testament, as did Plato and the other philosophers, who were much later in time than Moses. Whatever truth there was in them ultimately came from the biblical revelation. Justin argued that if they adopted Christianity, pagans would be able to see the whole truth that lay behind their very partial grasp of it. The light of Christ had come into the world and removed the darkness of paganism, but sadly, too many pagans were blind to it.

Tertullian of Carthage was another writer of this period who wrote against both Jews and pagans, and his arguments were very similar to Justin's. Tertullian also wrote against the Gnostics, and in this he was consciously following Irenaeus of Lyon (c. 135–202), who compiled an encyclopedic work titled *Against Heresies*, in which he attacked their pseudo-Christian religious systems. The Gnostics wanted to pick and choose elements of Jewish and/or Christian thinking, which they then wove into a mix of truth and error that was based more on fantasy than on fact, but Irenaeus and Tertullian wanted consistency—they believed that the Bible made sense on its own and that it could not be quarried for ideas that could then be taken out of context and used to support something quite different from God's self-revelation. Tertullian went even further and wrote a book about it (*Prescription against Heretics*), in which he argued that a heretic was unable to interpret the Bible correctly because he did not have the mind of the Holy Spirit who wrote it. In other words, you have to be in tune with the author of the message if you hope to understand it.

Tertullian's Montanist sympathies came out most clearly in his moral treatises, where he offered practical advice to Christians in the conduct of their daily affairs. In particular, he claimed that the Mosaic law had not been abolished by the coming of Christ so much as strengthened and made more demanding. For example, where matrimony had been permitted and encouraged in the Old Testament, it was still permitted in the New but married couples ought to forswear sexual intercourse and the begetting of children because the end of time had come and there would be no future generations. Similarly, Tertullian extended Paul's command for married women to cover their heads to virgins as well, arguing that the apostolic precept was intended to apply to all women and not just to wives. His basic principle was that the New Testament represented a transition from the old dispensation to the new, and therefore allowed a certain laxity in areas like these until such time as the people were ready to accept stricter measures. The coming of the Holy Spirit (the Paraclete) to Montanus and his companions was the sign that the period of transition had come to an end and that the spiritual power to achieve perfection, missing from the law and only partly given by Christ and his apostles, had at long last arrived. It was this relegation of the New Testament to a secondary status, and the corresponding elevation of the Montanist prophecies to the level of a third and definitive divine revelation, that the church was forced to reject and that made Tertullian suspect, though he was never declared a heretic and his writings continued to be read, if not followed, in these particular areas.

Tertullian is also the main source for our knowledge of Marcion, whose reductionist and anti-Jewish form of Christianity he attacked in no fewer than five books, the longest of his many surviving works. In the course of this extended argument he gives us the fullest exposition of the relationship between the Old and New Testaments to come from the early church period, and shows how the latter cannot be understood without the former.

We can therefore conclude that by about the year 220 at the latest, Christians had articulated and defended the following main points in their understanding of the Bible:

1. The New Testament is the fulfillment of the Old.

2. The Old Testament must be read as a Christian book, preparing the way for the coming of Christ.

3. Pagan religions and philosophies were pale versions, and even corruptions, of God's revelation in the Old Testament, which was their ultimate source.

These three principles were to guide all subsequent patristic biblical interpretation in the context of evangelism to Jews and pagans.

### The Beginnings of Christian Biblical Interpretation

The approach of the second-century apologists was continued by Clement of Alexandria (c. 150–215), the first Christian writer who practiced what we would now recognize as biblical interpretation, but in his comments on the Bible (*Hypotyposes*) he confined himself to interpreting a few selected passages in an allegorical manner that sometimes verged on fantasy, not to say heresy.[27] It was left to Origen, one of Clement's pupils, to develop biblical interpretation in a systematic way. Origen's literary output was so enormous and varied that, had it survived intact, it would be the largest body of literature to have come out of the early church. Unfortunately, about 150 years after his death some of his ideas became suspect and his reputation suffered. A further 150 years after that, his writings were condemned and they were either destroyed or no longer copied, though by then there were a number of Latin translations. Most of them were done around AD 400 by Jerome and his colleague Rufinus of Aquileia, who was one of Origen's great admirers, and they have survived.

---

27. Only a few fragments survive, but it was known to Photius in the ninth century, who had a poor opinion of it. (Photius, *Bibliotheca*, 109).

Origen's influence on biblical interpretation, especially in the Greek-speaking world, was all-pervasive. For more than a century after his death there was nothing to compare with his work, and when later fathers started commenting on the Bible again, recycling his ideas was standard practice. Much of what they wrote can probably be traced back to Origen's influence even if it is not directly attributable to him. As time went on, however, the inadequacies and inner contradictions of Origen's approach could not be ignored, and a reaction set in. The history of patristic biblical interpretation can largely be written in terms of the degree to which the fathers distanced themselves from him. A few stayed close to the master, but the majority moved off in a different direction, albeit in different ways and to differing degrees. By the fifth century there were very few Origenists among the fathers and several of them were openly opposed to him, yet paradoxically they were all indebted to his work one way or another.

### The Greek Tradition

Origen had been educated in Alexandria, and it has often been assumed that later fathers with a similar background followed his hermeneutical methods in what was supposedly an Alexandrian school of interpretation. But early in his career Origen had fallen out with the church in his home city and had moved to Caesarea Maritima in Palestine, where he established his famous school and did most of his work on the Bible. His approach may have been typically "Alexandrian" in the sense that it followed principles laid down by his predecessors in that city, but his methods were not perpetuated there after his death. Later Alexandrian writers were no more dependent on (or independent of) him than anyone else. There were political rivalries between Alexandria and Antioch, the other great city of the Greek-speaking East, and in the early fifth century these spilled over to Constantinople, the capital of the Roman Empire established by the Emperor Constantine I in 330, but these were not the result of different schools of biblical interpretation. There is a sense in which Alexandria and Rome lined up against Antioch and Constantinople in the great theological debates that marked the period from the First Council of Nicaea in 325 to the Council of Chalcedon in 451. Naturally each side in these debates appealed to the Bible in support of its position on different matters relating to the Trinity and the human nature of Christ, but it cannot be said that there were rival schools of biblical interpretation that fueled these controversies.

Nor would it be right to say that the Alexandrians were Origenists who came out of the quarrels as orthodox and that the Antiochenes were condemned as heretics because they rejected Origen's spiritual hermeneutics in favor of a more literal exegesis. Some Alexandrians were always considered orthodox (like Athanasius and Didymus the Blind), while others were denounced as heretics (like Arius and Apollinarius). Likewise, some Antiochenes were revered as staunch defenders of orthodoxy (like John Chrysostom) while others were accused of heresy (like Nestorius), but biblical interpretation in both places managed to flourish as a discipline over and above the doctrinal disputes in the church.

Cyril of Alexandria and his Antiochene contemporary Theodoret of Cyrrhus (c. 393–466) both produced notable works of biblical exegesis, and neither was Origenist in his approach. Theodore of Mopsuestia (c. 350–428), the greatest of the Antiochene commentators, was anti-allegorical (and therefore regarded as anti-Origenist) in outlook, but his writings were acceptable to Cyril. As with Origen, a good portion of his work was translated into Latin. Ironically, he was condemned by the church at the same time as Origen (in 553), despite the fact that his biblical hermeneutic was very different. His commentaries were no longer copied in Greek, though, as with Origen, the Latin translations have survived, in his case under the name of Ambrose of Milan, whence they were transmitted to the Middle Ages as standard works of biblical interpretation. After the Council of Chalcedon many of Theodore's writings were translated into Syriac on the ground that they were Nestorian, while Cyril's commentaries appeared both in Syriac and in Armenian because they were thought to be Monophysite, a circumstance that inevitably lent credibility to the idea that there was a great rivalry between Alexandrian and Antiochene exegesis, but this manufactured opposition has no basis in the texts themselves.[28]

There were also Greek-speaking commentators on Scripture who were neither Alexandrian nor Antiochene, like the Cappadocian fathers, of whom the best known were Basil of Caesarea (c. 329–379), Gregory of Nazianzus (c. 330–390), and Gregory of Nyssa (c. 330–395). None of these was primarily a biblical scholar, but all wrote on parts of Scripture in ways that are similar to their contemporaries, though not obviously dependent on them.

Later on, when Procopius of Gaza (c. 465–528) and others set out to compile anthologies of the best Greek commentators in their *catenae* ("chains"), they drew on the full range of authors available to them, including Origen, and showed no sign of leaning toward one school of interpretation over against the other. Where the reading of

---

28. Nestorius was accused of holding that the incarnate Christ had two natures (divine and human) that were only superficially united in a single "person" (appearance), whereas the Monophysites believed that the human nature of Jesus was absorbed into his divine nature by the agency of the divine person of the Son of God. The Council of Chalcedon decreed that the Monophysites were right about the unity (and agency) of the Son's person but that the Nestorians were correct to maintain that the incarnate Christ had two natures that did not mix and mingle. As so often happens in situations like this, a solution that was intended to bring two approaches together ended up creating three—the Nestorian, the Monophysite, and the Chalcedonian. The Western churches (Catholic and Protestant) and what we call the "Greek" Orthodox Church are all Chalcedonian.

the Bible is concerned, the evidence points to both a diversity and a unity in the Greek-speaking Christian world that cannot be reduced to an Alexandria-Antioch rivalry or interpreted exclusively in the light of the Council of Chalcedon.

## The Latin Tradition

In the Latin West, serious commentary writing did not begin until after AD 350. The most outstanding figure, comparable in some respects to Origen, was Jerome, who translated the Bible into Latin and commented on it as he went along. Jerome started off as one of Origen's great admirers, but as he penetrated the subject more deeply, he realized that Origen was in many respects misguided and his initial devotion turned to deep-seated antipathy. This was unfortunate for his relationship with his colleague Rufinus, who did not give up on Origen and whose translation work has preserved much of what Origen wrote. Western writers were familiar with their Greek counterparts to some degree, but they went their own way.

Augustine of Hippo, the most prolific and renowned of the Latin fathers, was not a great biblical commentator, though he did write extensively on the Psalms and on John, but he was important as a theorist of biblical interpretation. His book *Christian Instruction* is one of the most important manuals of biblical hermeneutics ever written, and it is still widely read today. It is perhaps indicative of the complexity of the world in which Augustine lived that he got a substantial portion of his ideas from Tyconius, a Donatist schismatic, and that he ended up condemning Pelagius, one of the greatest biblical commentators of his time. Biblical interpretation transcended the limits of church politics and doctrinal controversy.

Ambrose of Milan (c. 339–397) was a popular biblical commentator, so much so that the works of Ambrosiaster and Theodore of Mopsuestia (in translation) were attached to his name. His own output was less distinguished than theirs, but because of the confusion just mentioned, he got the credit for works that were not his and was more highly regarded in later ages than he should have been. Latin commentary writing went on without interruption into the eighth century, the outstanding figures being Gregory the Great (c. 540–604) and the Venerable Bede, who aimed to comment on the entire Bible and whose work, heavily dependent as it was on his Latin predecessors, became a standard reference tool throughout the Middle Ages.

*Oriental Traditions*

The Armenian, Georgian, Coptic, and Ethiopian churches all have biblical commentaries from ancient times, though most of them are translations from Greek. Their main importance is that they preserve texts of the Greek fathers that are otherwise lost. The most productive of these languages was Syriac, which maintained a vigorous literature until the ninth century or even later. Once again, there are many translations from Greek, but the Syriac fathers also produced a large quantity of original works. The best known of them was Ephraim (Ephrem) the Syrian (c. 306–373), whose work was so good that it was translated into Greek—a rare honor—and praised even by as demanding a critic as Jerome. Much of what is attributed to him is not authentic, but his genuine writings are of considerable interest. Unusually, Ephraim preferred to write in poetry and he had a special affinity for Jewish exegesis, partly due to his use of Syriac (Aramaic), which gave him a deeper insight into Hebrew than was common among the fathers.

After the Council of Chalcedon most Syriac writers became either Nestorian or Monophysite, which effectively meant that they would not be translated into Greek, and this limited their circulation.[29] It is

---

29. Both Monophysites and Nestorians flourished in the Syriac-speaking world, with the result that biblical commentaries reflecting both positions were either composed from scratch or translated from Greek.

only in modern times that a knowledge of them has started to spread outside their home areas, and it must be said that appreciation of them is still quite limited. The recent emigration of many of these oriental Christians from their Middle Eastern homelands to Western countries, in particular to France and the United States, has encouraged the translation of their writings into French and English and assured them a modest but honorable place among the traditional fathers of the church.

*Conclusion*

We come back now to the question with which we began: Who exactly are the church fathers? The traditional definition, based on the criterion of theological orthodoxy, is necessary for understanding the doctrines of the church, but it is not adequate for describing patristic biblical interpretation, which goes beyond the bounds of ecclesiastical orthodoxy. Schismatics like Tyconius and heretics like Pelagius must be given their due, however disconcerting that may be to some. Without passing judgment on their overall beliefs, we must admit that they were capable of making insightful remarks on particular passages of the Bible and that some of their opinions have survived the test of time, not least because they were recycled by (or under the names of) indisputably orthodox writers. Likewise, we have to accept that even the most orthodox could go wrong and that they sometimes did—not even the brilliance of Augustine or Chrysostom could preserve them from occasional error. Nor are we in a position to criticize the ancients indiscriminately. Sometimes we can say with some assurance that they were wrong about certain things, but there are other times when they may have seen matters more clearly than we do, not least because their perspective was different from ours. Evaluating their interpretations of the Bible must therefore be a cautious exercise, undertaken in humility and respect for their world-changing achievement. For when all is said and done, the fathers moved the world of antiquity away from its inherited paganism to Christianity, a shift that was to be fundamental in the construction of our own civilization. They are voices from the past to be sure, but they have not been drowned out by modernity, and for those who have ears to hear, they can still convey to us what the Holy Spirit is saying to the church.

### WHAT IS BIBLICAL INTERPRETATION?

The most basic difference between the world of pagan antiquity and that of the early church lies in their very different perceptions of what constitutes the source of truth. For the pagans, this was a mixture of inherited tradition and speculation. The city-states of Greece and Rome looked back to their semi-mythical origins and maintained rituals that were supposed to protect them against all comers, though whether those rituals were up to the task allotted to them was not obvious, and the rationale behind them was increasingly questioned as time went on. Why should a city maintain temples and authorize sacrifices to gods who behaved capriciously and who might even be at odds with one another? That made no sense, and the philosophies of ancient Greece arose as attempts to replace this kind of "religion" with more rational explanations of the universe. But the philosophers did not really know any more than the rest of the population, despite their claims to intellectual superiority.

In contrast to this, the Christian church proclaimed an understanding of the world that it had received by divine revelation. This revelation was not purely theoretical but had been worked out in the history of Israel, which the church claimed as its own inheritance. Access to it was relatively easy and open to the public. It was not necessary to have exceptional intellectual ability in order to understand it, nor was it encumbered with ancient and incomprehensible traditions that made no sense. The world was part of a coherent universe that had been made by a good God. It had fallen under the dominion of evil spiritual forces whom God had created good but who had rebelled against him, tempting human beings to follow suit. God could have rejected humans, but instead he chose to become one of them, to take their rebellion upon himself, to pay the price demanded for it, and to save those who believed in him. Unlike the philosophers, Christians knew in whom they had believed, and had the key to understanding his purposes for them. The words of the prophets and apostles who had proclaimed that message had been written down so that it might be better understood and disseminated equally to everyone.

All that was required was to hear the message, accept its truth, and put it into practice. Christians did not have to speculate about the nature of reality, because that was set out for them in the Bible. What they did have to do was learn how to understand the revelation that had been given to them. At one level it was clear enough and could be understood with little difficulty. But behind the letter of the text lay a deeper spiritual meaning that could be discerned only by those whose minds were in tune with the Holy Spirit who had given the revelation. God had spoken to his people, but his words needed to be interpreted by those who were able to do so. Their interpretations were rational and were meant to have a practical application, but their reasoning was determined by the mind of God, and any consequences for behavior had to conform to the purposes for which that divine mind had created the world.

The mind and purposes of God revealed in the Scriptures had to be spiritually discerned and communicated to his people by those who had the gift of prophecy. Preaching and teaching were the appointed means for doing this, but the methods the preachers and teachers used had their own internal logic, and the forms in which the results were communicated corresponded to the gifts that they were given. Whole new genres, like textual commentary and sermons, came into existence, as did hermeneutical treatises designed to explain how the right meaning could be extracted from the sacred texts—and who was entitled to extract it.

In the nature of things, most of what was said and done in the early church is no longer accessible to us because it was not recorded or preserved. What we have are the written remains of a vast oral culture. Some of these remains have survived more or less accidentally and have little more than curiosity value, but for the most part they were deliberately set down so that future generations would know how to go about the task of proclaiming the message and what the results were likely to be. To unlock what they wanted to say, we have to examine the methods they followed and the modes of communication they employed. These may be set out according to the following pattern.

*Hermeneutical Theory*

There is a small but very important category of treatises that were written to explain what the rules and principles of biblical interpretation are (or were). They are the place we must start, because unless we understand where the fathers were coming from, we shall find it very difficult to appreciate what they were saying and almost impossible to evaluate their work objectively. The earliest was Tertullian's *Prescription against Heretics*, in which he argues that heretics cannot interpret Scripture correctly because they are not in tune with the Spirit of the God who revealed it. This is another way of saying that the Bible belongs to a community of faith and can be properly understood only within it. It does not mean that the community created the Bible, as many theologians have tried to argue, but rather that both the revelation and its interpretation were spiritual gifts that complemented each other, just as speaking in tongues required interpreters to make it meaningful (1 Cor 14:13–19).

The next stage of development comes with Origen's *First Principles* 4.1–3, three sections of a much longer theological treatise in which he expounds the levels of meaning that a biblical text can have. That idea is taken further and developed by Augustine in his *Christian Instruction*. Like all the fathers, Augustine regarded Christian doctrine and the message of Scripture as one and the same, and he set about explaining how exegesis of a text was meant to lead to an orthodox confession of faith. If it did not, then there was something wrong with the method or else the text itself was faulty, a possibility for which he was well prepared. Lastly there was Tyconius's *Book of Rules*, which is now lost but whose main points were preserved by Augustine and given an orthodox seal of approval that they might not otherwise have had.

## Exegesis

Exegesis was the earliest form of Christian commentary, represented by Clement of Alexandria and also by Origen, though most of what they wrote is no longer extant. By exegesis we mean simple explanations of unusual words, translations of Hebrew names (which often have theological significance), and so on. As time went on, this kind of material was incorporated into commentaries, which became the main vehicle for biblical interpretation generally. Later writers like Augustine made use of a question and answer format as a means of identifying textual difficulties and answering them without having to resort to a lengthy exposition of the passages concerned.

## Exposition

Exposition is an analysis of the biblical text that can be found in commentaries, which were pioneered by Origen but became frequent after AD 350, and also in many surviving sermons. The commentaries go through books of the Bible line by line and aim to give theological explanations of the texts. Some of them are quite brief, but others contain a large amount of information, ranging from detailed explanations of the Trinity to comments on laws and social customs that were unfamiliar and might be misunderstood by later generations of readers. Often the commentaries tell us more about the church in the time of the commentator than they do about the original context. A prime example of this is the way in which they generally handle 1 Corinthians 12 and 14, which regulate speaking in tongues and other spiritual gifts. We learn from the fathers that these gifts had effectively died out in their time, but most of them were careful not to reconfigure the text to make it refer to something else. Even though they did not always understand why things had changed over time, they recognized that they had and dealt with these vanished phenomena as best they could.

## Application

Application is found mainly in the sermons, or homilies, that have been preserved. Origen, John Chrysostom, and Augustine have all left major collections of these, and there are many others. A great deal of sermon material has been lost, and a rough estimate suggests that even in the case of Augustine we probably have no more than about 10 percent of what he preached. At the same time, there are many sermons attributed to him and to other famous fathers that are spurious, and it is anyone's guess where they may have originated. It is also uncertain what the relationship is between the written sermons that we possess and the oral delivery that supposedly lies behind them. In some cases it seems that the fathers wrote sermons that they never preached, while in other instances what we have is a record taken down by one of the hearers (who may or may not have been asked to do it). There is also the possibility that a sermon was preached and then edited by the preacher for publication. Sometimes we can tell what the most likely scenario is, but often we have to guess, and so the material has to be read with some caution.

A substantial number of sermons come from series preached on particular books of the Bible. This is particularly true of John Chrysostom, who worked his way through Matthew and John as well as the entire Pauline corpus (including Hebrews). In the case of Origen, we have many sermons on Old Testament books, including the Pentateuch, Joshua, Judges, and the Song of Songs, as well as on the Gospel of Luke in the New Testament.

### Allusions

Allusions are references to biblical texts in works that were written for some other purpose. It was common for the fathers to make a point in a treatise or book about something not directly related to the Bible and then back up what they were saying by quoting or alluding to a scriptural text. The relevance of the quotation or allusion is not always clear, and so we must be particularly careful in using this kind of source to generalize about the writer's approach to biblical interpretation. Allusions are by their nature extremely varied and variable and must be treated with caution. However, they have some use in helping us determine which books were considered to be authoritative Scripture and which were not, something that is particularly useful when dealing with texts that do not have many (or even any) commentaries on them.

### Anthologies

Anthologies are collections of biblical commentaries, of which the catenae are the most important. Very often they contain material that has otherwise been lost, and they tell us what ancient anthologists thought was particularly useful to preserve and to pass on to pastors and others who needed a handy reference guide for their own ministry.

*Miscellaneous*

The miscellaneous category is by definition open-ended but includes major works like Augustine's *City of God*, which is not biblical interpretation in the strict sense but a rewriting of world history on the basis of the Bible, which makes it relevant for understanding the way the Scriptures were read and understood. The category includes any number of other works, including poems based on biblical stories. This kind of material obviously has to be used with discrimination, but it can be valuable in helping us to understand the mentality of the fathers and gives us some idea of how deeply the Bible penetrated the thought world of the early church beyond the confines of public worship and proclamation.

SUMMARY

We can now summarize our findings as follows:

1. The church fathers normally used the Septuagint as their Old Testament text. Jerome did his best to persuade the Latin world to accept a translation based on the Hebrew, but he was only partially successful. On the other hand, the surviving commentaries and sermons avoid the so-called apocryphal books, which apparently were not much used in the church. The first person to write a commentary on any of them was Bede, at the very end of the patristic period, and even he seems to have limited himself to a single book—Tobit.

2. Every early Christian writer made some effort to interpret the Bible, which they all regarded as the source of Christian truth and teaching. Not all of these men

qualify as "fathers" of the church because some were schismatics or condemned as heretics, but to the extent that their biblical commentaries have survived, they must be included in any survey of patristic biblical interpretation. This is all the more so in that their works were mostly preserved by being passed off as the writings of genuinely orthodox commentators.

3. The fathers understood the importance of hermeneutical theory, and some wrote important treatises on the subject. For the most part, our access to their interpretation of the Bible is rooted in their commentaries and sermons. Relatively few of the latter have survived, but among those that we possess are several series on books of the Bible, and they give us a good idea of how the fathers sought to apply the text to their congregations.

# II

## THE CLASH of WORLDVIEWS

### CHRISTIANS IN DIALOGUE
### WITH JEWS AND PAGANS

Everybody in the ancient world knew that Jews were different from other people. As strict monotheists, they were religiously exclusive in a way that other nations did not understand and found hard to accept. A polytheistic society can always add extra gods to its pantheon, and this was often done. Around 164 BC Antiochus IV Epiphanes, the Hellenistic ruler of Syria and Palestine, tried to erect a statue of Zeus in the temple at Jerusalem, no doubt thinking that the Jewish God was just a different form of the Greek deity. The result was a national rebellion that led to the recovery of Jewish independence for the next century, when the country came under the sway of Rome. The Romans probably thought much the same thing about Judaism as Antiochus had done, but they were wise enough not to press the point. At the trial of Jesus,

Pontius Pilate did all he could to avoid getting involved in a Jewish religious dispute because he knew that it was more trouble than it was worth. Later on, when the apostle Paul fell out with Jewish leaders because of his preaching, the state authorities took a similar approach. Neither Paul nor the Jews made much sense to them, and they did what they could to stay out of the quarrel. When the Jews of Rome started arguing about the claims of Christ, the Emperor Claudius expelled them in order to preserve the city's peace. Jews were tolerated as long as they kept quiet, but they were not understood, nor were their theological disputes considered significant.

For their part, the Jews practiced as much social distancing from others as they could. In Palestine that was relatively easy because they were the majority of the population. Elsewhere it was more difficult, but if they were sometimes forced to compromise, they nevertheless did what they could to maintain their distinctiveness. The Romans did not erect temples to specifically Roman gods in the lands that they conquered, but the Jews built synagogues wherever they went and worshiped separately. More than that, they were happy to explain why they did so. From the days of their exile in Babylon, they made it clear to their pagan neighbors that they worshiped their own God because he was the only one who deserved it. The gods of Assyria, Babylonia, and Persia were nonentities, and to bow down to wood and stone images of them was the height of folly. Worse, it was blasphemy, because it meant worshiping created things instead of the Creator.

The Jewish priestly caste was also unlike anything in the pagan world. Jewish priests performed temple sacrifices much as their pagan counterparts did, but they were also intellectuals in a way that pagan priests were not. In the Greco-Roman world intellectuals tended to be anti-religious, viewing temple practices as irrational superstitions, but Jewish leaders thought that faith and philosophy were essentially the same thing. In the words of Psalm 19:7,

> The law of the LORD is perfect,
>     reviving the soul;
> the testimony of the LORD is sure,
>     making wise the simple.

Some pagans were impressed by this combination of piety and reason and were attracted to Jewish beliefs, though relatively few became converts. This was not for what we would call theological reasons—most of these people, whom the Jews called God-fearers, were quite happy to accept the main principles of Jewish theology. The problem was that to become Jewish involved more than just adopting a new set of beliefs. The potential convert also had to adopt a different way of life, governed by food laws and other restrictions that posed a formidable challenge to those who were not used to them and who failed to see why they were so important. For men, it meant being circumcised, which was painful for an adult and liable to expose him to ridicule among his peers. Jews were an ethnic minority, and while ethnic minorities can dissolve themselves in the wider population, the reverse is much harder—and therefore rare. Nor were Jews especially welcoming to outsiders. Like white people who attend a black church in modern America, the God-fearers might be perfectly acceptable as adherents but not encouraged to become members of the congregation, because if too many of them did so, the identity of the host community would be lost. We have to admit that the Jews had a point. When the Christian church broke down these ethnic barriers, the God-fearers flooded in and within a generation they had taken over. By AD 100, Jewish Christianity, dominant in the New Testament period, had all but disappeared.

By then, of course, the early church had developed its own approach to the Hebrew Bible, which continued to serve as its sacred Scriptures, even though the books of the New Testament were beginning to take their place alongside them. Jews and Christians agreed that the Hebrew Bible was the word of God, inspired by the Holy Spirit, revealed by the work of holy men of old, and given for the instruction of God's people (2 Pet 1:21; 2 Tim 3:16). Where they differed was in the way in which they interpreted it. Jews continued to regard it as God's law, meant to be fulfilled by them in detail, even after the destruction of the Jerusalem temple in AD 70. The disappearance of the daily sacrifices required considerable adaptation on their part, but the practices of the synagogues had long been in place as a guide, and their teachers (rabbis) took the place of the priests and Levites who could no longer perform their duties in the customary manner. The result was the gradual emergence of what would become an enormous body of "case law," preserved in what we call the Mishnah and later in the Talmud. Scholars differ about the extent to which this was a consciously anti-Christian development, but Christians played no part in it, and as time went on they became increasingly ignorant of it.

This progressive estrangement was probably inevitable because Christian interpreters of the Hebrew Bible read the texts in the light of the revelation of Jesus Christ, whom Jews rejected as their Messiah. As Christians understood it, the Old Testament spoke about Jesus in the sense that it was a collection of prophecies that foretold his coming. The Jewish laws illustrated how Christ would deal with the problem of sin and redemption. By becoming both the great high priest of Israel and the sacrificial victim who paid the price of sin once and for all, Jesus vindicated the truth of the Hebrew revelation and made it redundant at the same time. The fact that the temple had been destroyed was confirmation of this, because its rituals and sacrifices were no longer necessary. Jews had no answer to that other than to hope for the rebuilding of the temple at some future time, but Christians could claim that the Scriptures had been fulfilled in the life, death, and resurrection of Christ, making the temple and its sacrifices redundant. To them, the law of Moses was no longer applicable in physical terms, but it remained fully valid at the spiritual level because the ascended and glorified Christ continued to perform the law's requirements even as he sat at the right hand of his Father in heaven.

To the early Christians, therefore, a spiritual interpretation of the Hebrew Bible was the only one that made sense. The letter of the law, to which the Jews obstinately clung, was obsolete, but the spiritual principles that the law taught were fully manifested in Christ and were brought to life in the Christian by the indwelling presence of the Holy Spirit in the heart of every believer (Gal 4:6). In this way, Christians could claim that the Old Testament was actually more central to their religious beliefs and practices than it was to the Jews, making them, and not the adherents of rabbinic Judaism, the true Israel and the authentic heirs of the ancient Hebrew patriarchs and prophets.

This line of argument permeates Justin Martyr's *Dialogue with Trypho*, where he quotes numerous psalms, in addition to the prophets, as evidence not only that the historic Israel had failed to live up to the covenant that God had made with Abraham and Moses, but that the ancient covenant contained a built-in obsolescence that the coming of Christ has demonstrated and superseded. Consider the following:

> The lamb that God ordered to be sacrificed as the Passover was a type of Christ, with whose blood (in proportion to their faith in him) they anoint their houses (i.e., themselves), who believe in him. That the creation that God made—Adam—was

a house for the Spirit that proceeds from God is something you can all understand. That this injunction was temporary, I prove as follows. God does not allow the Passover lamb to be sacrificed in any place other than the one in which his Name was named, knowing that the days would come, after the suffering of Christ, when even that place in Jerusalem would be given over to your enemies, and all the offerings would cease. And that lamb that was commanded to be wholly roasted was a symbol of the suffering of the cross which Christ would undergo. For the roasted lamb is dressed up in the form of a cross. One spit is transfixed from the lower parts to the head, and one across the back, to which its legs are attached.[1]

Here we can see clearly the various ways in which the early Christians tackled the Jewish Passover tradition. The lamb was a type of Christ and his suffering, something that Justin claimed was prefigured in the fact that the roasted lamb was dressed up in the shape of a cross. The sacrifice could only be properly accomplished in Jerusalem, which would eventually be destroyed, proving that it was not intended to be of eternal significance. Finally, Christians applied the Passover to themselves in a spiritual way by claiming the protection of Christ's blood over them individually in a way that is analogous to the actions of the Hebrews on the night of the first Passover. What Jews commemorated as a distant historical event, Christians appropriated as an ongoing principle of their own spiritual lives, giving Passover a contemporary relevance that was essentially foreign to Judaism.

From a modern perspective, we would probably find the detail about the roasted lamb being dressed in the shape of a cross somewhat odd if it were to be used as evidence pointing to the sufferings of

---

1. Justin Martyr, *Dialogue with Trypho* 40.

Christ. But other aspects of Justin's argument may be more appealing, especially the assertion that Christians are delivered from death by the blood of Christ in a way that is not dissimilar to what happened to the Hebrews at the first Passover. This is an illustration rooted in spiritual principle, not a similarity based on physical coincidence, and the fact that it is more likely to carry conviction with modern believers underlines the church fathers' basic contention—that the Old Testament law must be read and applied to Christ in a spiritual manner.

The early Christians also interpreted many of the people and incidents found in the Hebrew Bible as signs of the Messiah who was to come. This way of reading the text was common to the New Testament writers, especially to the apostle Paul and the writer to the Hebrews, who made frequent references to Old Testament characters like Abraham, Moses, and Melchizedek as men who in different ways prefigured Christ. Later generations continued this way of thinking and developed it further. Justin Martyr, for example, drew a parallel between Mary, the mother of Jesus, and Eve, the wife of Adam. According to him, both women were virgins who conceived, but whereas Eve brought forth disobedience and death because she listened to the serpent, Mary gave birth to the God-man "in order that the disobedience which proceeded from the serpent might be destroyed in the same way in which it derived its origin."[2] This comparison and contrast came to be known as recapitulation (*anakephalaiosis*), a process by which everything that had gone wrong in the descent of Adam was put right by the coming of Christ.

The pattern was not developed systematically, but it was generally consistent in the sense that what appeared as types and shadows in the Hebrew Bible was revealed in its fullness by the

---

2. Justin Martyr, *Dialogue with Trypho* 100.

gospel. This typology, as it is now called, was characteristic of the church fathers and is often confused with allegory, but it is not the same. Typological interpretation accepts the historicity of the Old Testament accounts but sees them as pointing to a future fulfillment that goes far beyond what was revealed to the Jewish prophets and patriarchs. Allegory, on the other hand, generally assumes that the written account was never meant to be read literally as a historical narrative but was always intended to be read in a metaphorical sense. Where the boundary lay between typology and allegory was not always clear, and some texts were hard to categorize. The Song of Songs, for example, could be read as an allegory and not as a historical account, but what about Genesis 3? The Song might be seen as a picture of the spiritual union between Christ and the church that all Christians are called to experience. Genesis 3, on the other hand, describes a real event that was put right—recapitulated—by the death and resurrection of Jesus, an event that all Christians believed was literally true, however stylized and symbolic the presentation of the fall of humanity might be.

Persuading Jews to read their Scriptures in this way was no easy task and could succeed only if the Jews in question were predisposed to a messianic interpretation of their faith. Those who were then had to be persuaded that the Messiah they longed for had already come, even though the kind of restored Israel that they had been led to expect had not materialized. There is little evidence that this strategy worked, because few Jews were persuaded by it. It seems more likely that the arguments used by Justin, and by others like Tertullian, who also wrote against Judaism, were more effective in dissuading gentiles from becoming God-fearers than they were in persuading Jews to accept the claims of Christ. In effect, what the Christians were saying is that pagans attracted to Judaism could have everything that the religion had to offer without any of the inconveniences that went along with it. Jewish intransigence on the need to uphold the physical details of the law was used by Christians as evidence that their priorities were wrong. In words attributed to Trypho, "You Christians expect to get good things from God but you do not keep his commandments. Have you not read that the soul that is not circumcised on the eighth day shall be cut off from his people? This has been ordained for foreigners and slaves, just as much [as for Jews]. You despise the covenant rashly, rejecting the duties it imposes on you, and yet try to persuade yourselves that you know God when in fact you do none of the things that a true God-fearer would do."[3] There is no reason to suppose that Justin was misrepresenting the Jewish position, which has remained constant down through the ages, and it is not surprising that gentiles would find the spiritual interpretation of the law put forward by Justin and his fellow Christians a more attractive option. Judaism would continue to attract gentiles as late as the fourth century, as we know from the sermons that John Chrysostom preached against it, but the arguments he used remained much the same as those employed by Justin more than two centuries earlier.

The later church fathers spent relatively little time justifying their interpretation of the Bible to Jews, partly because the topic was already well covered in the New Testament and partly because there were too few Jews to make the effort worthwhile. It was very different with gentiles, however. Christians could not assume any prior knowledge of the Scriptures among pagans, and there was no expectation that the Hebrew Bible would be highly regarded by them. On the contrary, most pagan intellectuals treated the Bible much as they did any non-Greek literature. They either ignored it or looked down on it as the inferior product of a barbarian mind. In dealing with them, therefore,

---

3. Justin Martyr, *Dialogue with Trypho* 10.

the Christians had to take an entirely different approach. Once again, Justin Martyr pointed the way in which this would be done.

The first principle that the Christians proclaimed was the superiority of reason, a belief that they were convinced most educated pagans would share with them. As Justin put it, "Reason directs those who are truly pious and philosophical to honor and love only what is true. ... It is incumbent on the lover of truth to choose to do and say what is right, even if he is threatened with death."[4] As Justin did not fail to point out, lovers of the truth are to be found in every nation, not just among the Jews, but they are persecuted because of it. The classic case was that of Socrates, who in many respects was similar to Jesus Christ and who suffered a comparable fate. But there was also a crucial difference between the two men. Justin wrote,

> No one trusted in Socrates to the point of dying for his doctrine, but in Christ, who was partially known even by Socrates (for he was and is the Word who is in every man, and who foretold the things that were to come to pass both through the prophets and in his own person when he was made of like passions, and taught these things), not only philosophers and scholars believed, but also artisans and people entirely uneducated, despising both glory and fear and death, since he is a power of the ineffable Father, not the mere instrument of human reason.[5]

It was in this way that the early Christians presented themselves as seekers after truth who were forced to suffer for their commitment to what is right, just as the most noble pagans had done before them. But great as these ancient heroes were, they were still inferior to the

---

4. Justin Martyr, *First Apology* 2.
5. Justin Martyr, *Second Apology* 10.

prophets of Israel, not least because they had borrowed all their best ideas from them: "And that you might learn that it was from our teachers that Plato borrowed his statement that God, having altered matter that was shapeless, made the world, hear the very words of Moses, who was the first prophet and of greater antiquity than the Greek writers, and through whom the Spirit of prophecy indicated how and out of what materials God first formed the world, spoke thus: 'In the beginning, God created the heaven and the earth.' "[6]

So, according to Justin, the Greek philosophers, and those who followed them, were basically indebted to the Hebrew Bible, even though they did not know it. Where they were blind was in the way that they tolerated pagan worship, which they knew was irrational. How could anybody make an idol out of stone or base metal and then bow down and pray to it? That made no sense. People like Socrates and Plato knew it, but they had nothing better to put in its place. On this subject the Old Testament prophets provided a rich source of invective, which men like Justin could use to make the same arguments against paganism that they did, from reason alone. As Justin and his fellow Christians understood it, the Hebrew prophets spoke with power because their words were not their own but came from God. The men whose words had instructed the Greeks had also predicted the coming of Christ, and the true philosopher would hear them speaking of him.[7] All truth is one, the main difference between the Greeks and the Hebrews being that the former received it in a partial and veiled manner whereas the latter got it directly from God, the source of all that is good, just, and true. Why settle for second best, Justin argued, when the fullness of divine truth was readily available in the Scriptures?

---

6. Justin Martyr, *First Apology* 59.

7. Justin Martyr, *First Apology* 31–53.

By adopting this approach, which was imitated by many others in the second and early third centuries, Justin and his successors honored the pagans for the good they had done but at the same time relegated them to a second tier and deprived them of their authority. In Justin's words, "On some points we teach the same things as the poets and philosophers whom you honor, and on other points we are fuller and more divine in our teaching."[8] That said it all.

In presenting their case to their pagan contemporaries, the early Christians seldom quoted the Bible directly, for the simple reason that they could not assume that their interlocutors knew it or would accord it any authority. But by undermining the authority of the pagan intellectual giants and insisting that the Bible was superior to them in every way, they created a climate in which their claims about Christ could be given serious consideration. This process took a couple of generations to mature, but by about AD 200 it had made enough progress for Christian writers to be able to expound the Scriptures in the expectation that their readers would not only understand them but also be prepared to hear from them what the truth actually was.

BIBLICAL PRINCIPLES:
WHAT THE CHURCH FATHERS WANTED TO TEACH

The church fathers saw themselves primarily as preachers and teachers of a faith that was radically different from the culture of the ancient Greco-Roman world. The principles of that faith were set out in the Bible, which made certain statements about the nature of reality that could not be ignored. Unless and until those basic principles were accepted, the preaching and spread of the gospel was impossible. Jesus had come to Israel, not to the gentiles, because

---

8. Justin Martyr, *First Apology* 20.

only Israel had the intellectual and spiritual preparation that made his mission meaningful. The first task of the fathers therefore was to get the gentile world to that point. As Christian apologists understood it, there were four main principles on which the biblical revelation was based—monotheism, creation, theodicy (the nature of evil), and eschatology—each of which had to be understood and accepted before Christianity could make serious headway.

## Monotheism

Monotheism is so obvious to Christians today that it is hard to realize that for most people in the ancient world it was a novelty. Even in relatively enlightened places like Athens there were altars and temples to any number of deities, as Acts 17:16 reminds us. Despite their dedication to philosophy, the Athenians were deeply superstitious, so much so that they had even erected an altar to the "unknown God," just in case (Acts 17:23). Paul, as we know, latched onto that and used it to preach Christ, whom he identified as this unknown one. This was a constant theme of early Christian evangelism. Pagans were blind to the truth because they did not know where to find it. As a result they seized on any number of crazy ideas and made little or no attempt to harmonize them. Instead, their gods were often in conflict with each other and were as liable to harm human beings as to help them.

The God of the Bible is not like that at all. Everything that exists was made by him and is preserved in existence by him. We may not know what his purposes are, but that he has a mind and a plan for his creation is clear from his revelation. The sovereignty of the one God gives coherence to the universe, eliminating conflict between different spiritual powers and ensuring that nothing is beyond his control. The gods of the other nations are but idols—this is a constant biblical refrain and it was constantly echoed in the writings of the church fathers. On this score, a man like Theophilus of Antioch (second century) was every bit as fierce in his denunciation of idolatry as any Old Testament prophet, and the same was true of Tertullian, who did not hesitate to deride the foolishness of the pagans.

The fathers were strong in their denunciation of a religiosity that made no sense. They appreciated the comprehensiveness and inclusivity of biblical monotheism, which helped them see that there is a universe in which all things work together for good to those who love God and are called according to his purpose, whether they are Jews or not. They were never afraid of being tripped up by some unknown deity whom they had forgotten to propitiate, because the God of the Bible is everywhere present— and in control. He can be worshiped by anyone and will pour out his blessings on all who believe in him, regardless of who they are or where they come from.

The fathers also understood that the God of the Bible is morally upright. Pagans often found themselves conflicted over this. They had a moral sense, which could often be quite strong and compelling, but their gods often did not. Like movie stars or pop idols today, the gods lived in a debauched world of their own, doing things that ordinary mortals would be ashamed of and that might well be illegal. How could such unworthy figures be the object of worship? The Christians' simple answer was that they could not, because they were figments of the human imagination and not real beings. Or if they did have some kind of reality, they were demons whose purpose was to deceive people, not to enlighten them. The God of the Bible is entirely different from that. To worship him is also to keep his law, and his law is the yardstick of morality.

This moral dimension of monotheism comes naturally to us, but ancient attitudes were very different. Even among Christians there were many who found it hard to reconcile the goodness of God with the evil of the material world around them. The idea that a good God would have created such a universe seemed incredible to them, and one solution that some came up with was to claim that the world was made, not by the Father of Jesus Christ, but by an inferior Creator God, known to us by the Greek term "Demiurge" (*Dēmiourgos*). What distinguished him was his inherent weakness. He could create a material world but could not make it perfect. It contains built-in flaws that have led to the proliferation of sin and evil, and that cannot be corrected other than by the intervention of a higher deity, who comes to us as our Redeemer. The Redeemer God, who is the Heavenly Father of Jesus, sent his Son into the created order, where he was attacked and put to death. But death could not hold him, and in his resurrection he triumphed over the Demiurge and all his works. Variations on this theme can be found in a number of second-century writers, whom we now group together as "Gnostics" because they believed that they possessed a higher knowledge (*gnōsis*) that told them these things.

Those who proclaimed this higher knowledge were inevitably inclined to reject what they saw as the gross materialism of the Old Testament. How could a spiritual Redeemer God be interested in what kinds of food people ate, or what types of sacrifice they offered? He was surely above such things, and some aspects of the teaching of Jesus and his disciples would appear to encourage that way of thinking. But whereas the Gnostics practiced various forms of asceticism in order to minimize the impact of the evil world upon them, Jesus taught that the creation was good and should not be avoided or despised. The Creator and the Redeemer are not two different deities, but one and the same God. This belief had momentous consequences for the way in which Christians perceived both creation and the nature of evil and had a controlling influence on their interpretation of the Bible.

*Creation*

The heart of biblical monotheism is found in the Ten Commandments (Decalogue), which were just as central to the Christian understanding of the Bible as they were for Jews. The first three commandments focus our attention on God, and the last six on our fellow human beings (or neighbors), each of whom had to be treated with the appropriate dignity and respect. Joining heaven and earth is the fourth commandment, commanding observance of the Sabbath day. The Sabbath is primarily about the nature and limits of creation—in six days God had made the heavens and the earth, and when his work was complete, he rested. The pattern of divine labor was to be imitated by human beings, who were also called to rest—and to worship their Creator—every seventh day. Life on earth was thus connected to life in heaven, and the one was a picture image of the other. This was to be a major element in the way that the fathers interpreted the Bible and applied it to the life of the church. The six days of Creation were a constant ingredient of their biblical interpretation and formed the basic structure within which their worldview was constructed.

Pagan religions had many and varied explanations for the existence of the world, all of which were no more than speculation and many of which had been mythologized in one way or another. Very often pagans concluded that matter was evil or corrupted in some way, and that explained why there were problems in the world. The biblical account is very different. God made the world in an order and with a plan. The human race is the crowning glory of his creation, and everything else was made for humanity's enjoyment and use. In effect the Bible teaches that there are scientific laws governing the universe—not because it says that explicitly but because the law of the Lord is apparent throughout the created order (Ps 19). Nothing is purely arbitrary, even if in the poor state of our knowledge there are many things that are inexplicable—to us.

The fathers were fascinated by the biblical doctrine of creation and wrote extensively on it. A whole genre of Christian literature grew up around the interpretation of Genesis 1–3. It explained in great detail what happened on each of the six days of creation, hence the name *Hexaemeron* ("six days") given to it. We know of at least twelve treatises that were written in this genre from about AD 200 onward, though only five are now extant in their entirety.[9] But that is only part of the story. Origen wrote no fewer than thirteen books on the subject of creation, which are now lost (apart from a few fragments), and also preached sixteen sermons on it, which survive. Several other commentaries were produced by later writers, most of which have disappeared, though a complete text of Didymus the Blind turned up in a collection of papyri discovered at Tura (Egypt) in 1941. There are two sets of sermons from John Chrysostom, commentaries by Jerome and Ephraim the Syrian, and no fewer than three distinct treatments by Augustine—four if we include the last three books of his *Confessions*.

Creation was such a popular topic because it was fundamental to the Christian worldview. The world is not an extension of God and cannot be regarded as in any sense a part of his own being. If that is so, then it must be completely different from him—temporal rather than eternal, finite rather than infinite, mortal rather than immortal. No creature could be worshiped as God, nor could God be contained in any physical object. Yet, at the same time, creation is good, neither evil in itself nor the source of evil. There is therefore no need to run away from it or to attempt to deny it. But although the fathers believed in the goodness of creation, they also valued asceticism—fasting, celibacy, and so on. It was not that there was anything wrong with food or sexual intercourse, but human beings

---

9. See C. Kannengiesser, *Handbook of Patristic Exegesis*, 2 vols. (Leiden: Brill, 2004), 1:278.

could easily be distracted by a desire for such things and lose sight of their spiritual duties. It was for that reason, and not because there was anything wrong with the creation itself, that they counseled people to avoid overindulgence in its delights.

It has to be said that the patristic doctrine of creation has come under fire in modern times, for at least two reasons. The first, which we have just mentioned, was the tendency to asceticism, which, despite all the justifications offered in support of it, was easily understood as world-denying. The imposition of celibacy, in particular, was greatly resented and frequently disregarded in later times, especially among morally minded people who could not accept the concubinage that often resulted among the officially celibate clergy. The other problem is that many of the fathers read the history of creation literally and believed that the world had been made about 4000 BC. They knew that much of the material in Genesis was symbolic, but they calculated the years literally—and sometimes rebuked pagans for thinking that matter was eternal, or at least much older than the Bible said it was. Today, most people think they were wrong about that, though they would also agree that the created order is temporal and not eternal. At the same time, the belief that matter can neither be created nor destroyed lends credibility to the idea that it is eternal, whether that is really the case or not.

From an outsider's point of view, Christianity first appeared to be a Jewish sect. When Paul evangelized in the Greek world and got into trouble, the Roman authorities regarded it as a quarrel among Jews. The same seems to have been true of pagans who objected to the preaching of the gospel on the ground that it was interfering with their religious practices—and profits derived from selling idols. But it was not long before it became clear that this pagan perception was a half-truth that was more likely to mislead observers than enlighten them. That Christians had a special relationship to

Jews was undeniable, but the signs that they were growing apart are already present in the New Testament. The fact that gentile converts to Christianity were not obliged to submit to Jewish laws like circumcision was one obvious sign that a parting of the ways was coming, even though some Jewish converts seem to have been able to maintain relations with their fellow Jews for a generation or more. Nevertheless, by the time the church fathers started writing, Judaism and Christianity were two different things and Christians were conscious of their need to distinguish them, not least in order to avoid seeing church members confronted with Jewish claims that they were not following God's word as they should.

At the heart of the difference was the understanding of creation. Christians fully accepted the Old Testament teaching on this subject, and to that extent were "Jewish" in their thinking. But Jews integrated the rhythms of their social and spiritual lives into the created order in a way that Christians did not. This was especially obvious in the observance of the food laws. These cut right across creation, with what was essentially an arbitrary divide. Jews were permitted to eat certain things and forbidden to eat others—not for any objective reason (like considerations of health or hygiene) but to reinforce their separate identity.[10] These laws, and the observances of ritual purity associated with them, were (and still are) integral to the Jewish perception of the world. Furthermore, Jews had no discernible eschatology. Many believed that the Messiah would come to redeem them at some point, but they seem to have conceived of this as the beginning of a golden age for them on earth, not as a winding up of the present age and the beginning of something entirely new.

---

10. Some modern interpreters try to explain the kosher laws in terms of health and hygiene, but they are fundamentally mistaken. The ancients did not think about such things in the way that we do.

Christians, on the other hand, believed that they were a "new creation" in Christ. This was symbolized by their choice of the first day of the week to replace the Sabbath. The first day was also regarded as the eighth—the day after the Sabbath and the beginning of a new work of God. It was not just the day of the first creation but also— and in some ways more significantly—the day of resurrection, the beginning of the new creation. It was not a day of total rest but one of worship of the Creator and Redeemer, an activity that demanded much more than mere physical labor.

But the real difference between the old and the new creation can be seen in the way Christians regarded the institution of matrimony. In the Old Testament marriage and procreation were of the utmost importance. Judaism was a family religion, and although it was possible to convert to it, most Jews were (or at least claimed to be) physically descended from Abraham. The long lists of genealogies in Genesis and in 1 Chronicles are there to prove it. So are the many prohibitions against marrying foreign wives—the bloodline (and therefore the faith) must not be corrupted by mixed marriages.

When we turn to the New Testament, the picture is very different. The only person with a genealogy to speak of is Jesus, and that was because he was born under the law and came to fulfill its promises. Christians were not against matrimony, but it can hardly be said that they encouraged it either. The reason for this was not some kind of prudishness about sex but that they saw themselves as a new and higher creation. They were no longer tied to physical descent but were the true children of Abraham, born of the Spirit. Christians could marry if they wished, and most did, but the real spiritual athletes remained celibate as both Jesus and Paul were. If there is one thing that united virtually all the church fathers, it was this. Hardly any of them were married, and most of them preferred celibacy as a surer pathway to the heavenly life.

The irony here, at least to modern minds, is that one of their favorite Old Testament books was the Song of Songs, which on the face of it is a poem (or series of poems) dedicated to extolling the joys of physical love. The fathers, however, almost uniformly saw it as an allegory of the relationship between Christ and his church, or else between Christ and the soul of the individual believer. Union with him was the ideal, and baptism replaced circumcision as the sign of entry into the covenant people of God. Circumcision placed the divine seal on the organ of human procreation, but baptism was the sign of a new and spiritual birth.

It is here perhaps more than anywhere that the difference in mindset between the fathers and the Jews, and also between the fathers and a majority of modern readers, is most acute. Few people today want to read the Song allegorically in the way the fathers did, but what other interpretation are they going to put on it? It is certainly not a hymn of praise to marriage, a social institution that is absent from the Song. Moreover, the message of the Song is that physical love wears out—it is given for a time and will be repeated in subsequent generations, but it is not meant to last forever. It brings great joy while it lasts, but heartache and longing when it goes away, as it inevitably does. The fathers knew this in their spiritual life with Christ. There were times when he seemed to desert them and they were put through what later mystics would call the dark night of the soul. But while they understood that Christian experience would have its ups and downs in this world, they also knew that the greatest joys we have here on earth are but a foretaste of the kingdom of heaven. The Song was therefore a promise of greater things to come, and read in that light, it fits perfectly into an overall hermeneutic of the Old Testament—the best is yet to be.[11]

---

11. Jews also allegorized the Song, but not in the christological way that is typical of Christian interpreters.

Modern readers do not like to hear that, but were the fathers so wrong? Given the transition from the old to the new creation, and the transformation that ensued in their reading of Scripture, can their perception of this gem of Hebrew poetry not be justified? Modern interpreters ought to be humble enough to recognize that the fathers' interpretation makes sense, given their presuppositions, and that history has shown the enduring appeal of their allegory. Even today when we sing "He brought me into his banqueting house, and his banner over me is love" (Song 2:4), how many people realize that this is the description of a seduction scene? Is it not true that almost everybody "gets it" as a description of how Christ demonstrates his love for us and brings us into his fellowship? And what is more, modern Christians do not have to be told that. Somehow the allegorical interpretation of the verse comes naturally, even to people who have no idea what its original context was.

In ancient times the only dissenter from the common opinion was Theodore of Mopsuestia, who claimed that the Song of Songs was an erotic love poem written by Solomon to counter the criticism he had received for marrying an Egyptian princess. A modern reader might sympathize with Theodore's view, but a little thought will show us that it is impossible. If Solomon had written it for the reason Theodore expressed, the Song would never have survived, because it was his foreign wives that turned him away from God to the worship of idols. No Jewish authority would have allowed that kind of thing to be celebrated, and they would certainly never have accepted it into the canon of Scripture. Even if Theodore was on the right track in rejecting allegory, his proposed alternative does not work, and we should not be too surprised that his view was explicitly condemned at the Second Council of Constantinople in 553.[12]

---

12. The condemnation was at the fourth session of the council, on May 12, 553. For the Latin text and translation, see John Behr, ed., *The Case against Diodore and Theodore: Texts*

The attitudes of the fathers toward marriage and celibacy are largely uncongenial to modern minds, but other aspects of their anti-Judaistic stance are regarded more favorably nowadays and need to be considered if a true picture is to be presented. One of these was their rejection of the physical dimension of ancient Israel. The fathers did not believe that the church needed to have a particular land to dwell in, a temple in which to worship God, or a political structure corresponding to that of David and Solomon. This became an important issue as the Roman Empire Christianized and its rulers began to demand a voice in church affairs. The belief that the church was the new Israel did not extend to the state, and no Christian ruler was entitled to claim the position of the ancient Israelite kings. There were times when such a fusion seemed likely, but it was always beaten back. Emperors occasionally tried to impose doctrinal formulations on the church, but if these did not accord with what church leaders themselves thought, they were resisted and eventually rejected. The new Israel was (and remained) a spiritual concept, and Christian rulers, as members of the church, were subject to its authority, not the other way round.

Also important, and of great relevance to the ordinary believer, Christians had a clear vision of what would happen to them after death. The Old Testament is vague on this subject. The dead are occasionally mentioned, but little is said about their state. That is not true of the New Testament, or of the early church. Christians were bound for heaven, for an eternal life of perfect joy in the presence of God. The present life on earth was not to be neglected, but it was to serve as a preparation for the eternity to come. For this reason, the church fathers felt obliged to give a spiritual interpretation to the law of Moses and to privilege it above the literal meaning. There were

---

*and Their Contexts* (Oxford: Oxford University Press, 2011), 414–17.

times, of course, where the practice of the literal sense had to be maintained—Christians were not allowed to commit murder, engage in adultery, or steal any more than Jews were. But Christians distinguished between crimes and sins. To kill another person was a crime, but to think evil of him in the heart was a sin. To put it a different way, all crimes were sins but not all sins were crimes. The law can only punish crimes, but God judges the secrets of the heart and metes out the same punishment on all sin. In this respect, the teaching of the New Testament and the interpretation of the fathers were of a different order to what the Hebrew Bible and the rabbis generally taught. Christians' focus was no longer on this world only but on the world to come, and that world was the one that counted more.

Some of the implications of the shift from the physical creation to the new creation took time for the fathers to absorb. One of these was the doctrine of election and predestination. Election was clear enough—the Christian church had simply replaced Israel as God's chosen people, and although God had not forgotten his promises to the latter, they would be fulfilled only in and through Christ. But predestination was another matter. Israel did not really have such a doctrine, partly because it lacked a developed eschatology but partly also because the entire nation of Israel was elect and therefore predestined, whatever that might mean. But Christians were not an elect nation in the same sense and could not rely on their human ancestry as justification for their eternal destiny. If they were chosen, it was because God had decided to do that, independently of their human origins.

### Theodicy

The unusual word "theodicy" describes the judgment or justice of God in the face of the existence of evil. What is evil and why does it exist? Pagans believed that it was the result of clashing forces. Some gods were good and others were not, so what could be attributed to the former was "good" and what belonged to the latter was not. Others thought of spirit as good and matter as evil. That was flatly contradicted by Genesis 1, where God surveyed all that he had made and pronounced it good, and also by the incarnation of the Son. Jesus Christ could not have existed had matter been intrinsically evil, because then he would have been partly evil himself, which he is not. But if evil is not present in matter, what is it? And why does a good God tolerate it?

There is no simple answer to these questions, which have been debated since ancient times, and we should not be surprised that the fathers failed to resolve them. But if they could not dispel every mystery, they could at least define the terms of the debate, and that they did very well. Because evil is not willed by God or created by him, it cannot be eternal. It can therefore be defeated and even eradicated, which is what the gospel of salvation is ultimately all about.

Evil is essentially a spiritual power. It is not present in matter, though evil forces can use the material creation for their own purposes. Nevertheless, they cannot transgress the bounds that have been placed on them by their own creation, and the children of God will not be overwhelmed by it. Evil is also personal in character—it came into being by the rebellion of the angel Satan, and it continues to be promoted by him. The struggle against evil is therefore a deeply personal one—as human beings we are either children of God or slaves of Satan. Salvation in Christ makes the former possible, but the latter state is the default position of humanity nowadays. The first human beings, Adam and Eve, were tempted by Satan to join his rebellion against the Creator, and the rest of us have inherited their sin. Here it is important to understand that, for the fathers, sinfulness is not an inescapable part of human nature but an unnatural imposition on it. Fallen humanity is not natural but unnatural—this is not the way we were meant to be. Salvation is therefore a healing, a restoration of what is abnormal to what God originally wanted for us. At the same time, it is more than that. Christianity is not a return to the garden of Eden but a progression to a higher life. Redemption is therefore not only greater than sin but greater even than creation itself.

It must be admitted that the fathers' understanding of evil was sometimes flawed because they equated goodness with God and therefore with perfect being. God was the one who is (*ho ōn* in Greek), and so evil was interpreted as the opposite of this—as nonbeing (*to mē on*). They did not always appreciate that spiritual goodness was manifested in obedience to God, making evil an expression of disobedience to him. Satan, for example, would not be called good merely because he was a creature, but he was not nonbeing either. His evil did not inhere in his physical structure but in his rebellion against God, and the same is true of human beings. Evil is not the absence of good but a powerful (and personal) force opposed to it. Failure to recognize this adequately led some of the fathers to downplay the reality of evil, with consequences that shaped their understanding of salvation.

Pagan philosophies and religions had tended to think of good and evil in terms of spirit versus matter. This was not entirely true; the Stoics and the Epicureans, for example, thought that everything, including spirit, was material—spirit being a highly refined and invisible form of matter. Nevertheless, for most pagans evil was rooted in matter, particularly of the grosser kind. To pursue the good was therefore to seek what is spiritual and to suppress the material. The fact that philosophers gave up worldly concerns in order to seek a higher wisdom was regarded as good, and the philosopher-king was held up as an ideal. The only person in patristic times who might plausibly be regarded as a philosopher-king was the emperor

Marcus Aurelius (r. 161–180), and some Christian writers appealed to him specifically. But Marcus Aurelius was hostile to Christians and persecuted them, because to his mind their understanding of good and evil was a perversion.

The biblical view is that evil is not part of creation but the result of a rebellion against the Creator. The fathers believed that the evil forces would be defeated, but not that they would be destroyed, because nothing that God made would perish completely. Instead, they insisted that those who had succumbed to evil would be eternally separated from God. That would be their punishment, though whether it would involve suffering was less clear. Evil was not natural or inevitable but rather a perversion that had no right to exist and that a sovereign God could not ultimately tolerate. In the biblical worldview, death was the consequence of evil at work in the world, but death is not the end of the human story. The message of the gospel is that death has been overcome by the resurrection of Jesus Christ, which is also the proclamation of the defeat of evil. The two forces are opposed in the world we live in, but not in the mind of God, who is sovereign over everything he has made, whether it is obedient to his will or not.

## Eschatology

Eschatology is the technical term for the future. Today we are used to thinking that the future will be better than the past, but that was not what most people in ancient times believed. On the contrary, they thought that the human race had started off in a golden age, which over time had progressively disappeared as sin took hold and twisted everything. The future could only be worse and was therefore something to be feared.

The Christian message was the exact opposite of that. Christians agreed that the world had been created good and that the first human beings had lived in a paradise, but they did not look at human history as an inevitable decline from that. Sin had certainly ravaged the human race, but there was a remedy—the atoning sacrifice of Jesus Christ and the promise of a fresh start. That was the good news of the gospel. Humanity was not fated to descend further and further away from the ideal. Those who trusted in Christ would not only be saved from that, but their lives would be transformed. This transformation would begin in this life but would not be brought to fruition until the return of Christ at the end of time.

What the gospel did was offer hope to the perishing. In a cruel world where disease, warfare, and famine took an annual toll of lives, the church held out a promise that the best was yet to come. The Bible is a book of prophecy, fulfilled to some extent (and in principle) by the death and resurrection of Christ, but pointing forward to the time when every knee will bow and every tongue confess that he is Lord (Phil 2:10–11) and when the kingdom of God will finally be revealed in power (1 Cor 15:28). Nobody knew when that would happen, but the signs of its coming were there. Miracles occurred, the gospel spread across the known world, and even the mighty power of Rome was laid low and forced to accept the spiritual rule of the one it had crucified. The end was clearly in sight, and when Rome fell to the barbarian armies of Alaric in 410, it seemed to many that it had arrived.

Up until then there had been a strong undercurrent in the church that looked forward to the imminent end of time. It was the spirit that motivated the Montanists in the second century and that appealed to Tertullian. The astonishing victories of the cross in the fourth century could only increase that feeling among many. And yet, when Rome fell, the reaction was quite different. Augustine of Hippo, appalled at what had happened, sat down to write his classic *City of God*, a major work of biblical interpretation that reordered the whole of human history from Adam and showed that Rome's fall was but the latest episode in an ongoing struggle that showed no sign of coming to an end. Using the biblical imagery of Babylon (the empires of this world) and Zion (the people of God), Augustine presented the church and wider Roman society with an understanding of events that has stood the test of time. His interpretation was not the death of apocalyptic theories proclaiming an imminent end—there are still people today who think like that—but it removed that kind of thinking from the mainstream of the church. Augustine's message was that human events mirror spiritual realities, but the two things are not to be confused. Christ will return like a thief in the night, when he is least expected, not when everyone thinks that the end is nigh.

Augustine's interpretation of eschatology is of a piece with the clear distinction between the secular and the spiritual that came to be the hallmark of patristic hermeneutics. To understand the Bible properly, the interpreter needs to have the mind of Christ and to see the unfolding of human history as a witness to God's saving grace, but not to regard it as an end in itself. The Roman Empire could never have been the kingdom of God on earth, but then neither could any of its successors. However "Christian" a state might be—or claim to be—it was only provisional, destined to rise and fall like other states and empires. The kingdom of Christ, when it came, would be something entirely new, not altogether unexpected perhaps, but unachievable in purely human terms.

## GRECO-ROMAN CULTURE:
### WHAT THE CHURCH FATHERS WANTED TO AVOID

Christianity made its appearance not in a primitive society or in a remote area but at the heart of a vibrant civilization that had recently been united under the aegis of the Roman Empire. By no means was everybody highly educated, and the majority of people were probably illiterate (certainly if women are included), but there was an active intelligentsia that the church had to wrestle with and win over if it could. There were some notable converts from paganism to Christianity, particularly in the fourth century, but there was always a hard core of elite opposition to the gospel that refused to go away. In the end, the emperor Justinian had to close the philosophical schools in Athens (AD 529), but even then the surviving pagan philosophers decamped to the Persian Empire, where they maintained a shadowy existence until the rise of Islam just over a century later. The enemies of Christianity were formidable and their influence was enduring. To combat them effectively the church fathers often had to use their arguments and "speak their language," as we would say today. How far this was a strategic necessity and how far it was a compromise with the ruling ideologies of the day is difficult to determine. Many modern scholars have decried the fathers' approach as the Hellenization of Christianity, the development of a dogmatic imperial church as opposed to the free society of brothers in Christ that had supposedly existed in earliest times.

This thesis was popularized by Adolf von Harnack (1851–1930), and its legacy is still apparent in some quarters, but few scholars today would be quite as categorical as he was. It is now generally understood that the fathers had to speak the language of their time, because if they had not done so, they would not have been understood. But to claim that they capitulated to a Hellenistic worldview is going too far. They moved in a culture permeated by Platonism (or more precisely by its descendant, Neoplatonism) and worked with similar concepts, but patristic Christianity was far from being Neoplatonic in content or in inspiration. The Neoplatonists of the time—Plotinus (204–270), Porphyry (234–305), and Proclus (412–485), for example—would certainly have recognized fellow travelers among the Christians if that is indeed what they had been, but they did not, and Porphyry in particular was deeply hostile to them. Clearly, a more profound analysis of the relationship between the fathers and the pagan culture of their time is required. We can set out the main points of divergence as follows.

### Philosophy versus Religion

In the ancient Greek world, philosophical schools were many and varied, but most of them were opposed to religion understood as a series of worship practices that had no logical basis. Plato even went so far as to want to abolish religion altogether on the ground that it was a superstition that had no place in a rationally ordered society. The biblical vision was completely different. In ancient Israel, wise men and priests went together, and the teaching of Christ was the true philosophy. Like the apostle Paul, the fathers were prepared to admit that Christian doctrine appeared to be foolishness to the world, but they insisted that in reality things were the other way round. "What has Athens got to do with Jerusalem?" was the famous question posed by Tertullian, but in saying that, he did not mean what many subsequent readers have supposed. Tertullian was not anti-intellectual but was basing his reasoning on the divine revelation in Scripture. What the Greek philosophers said came out of their own heads, but what Christian apologists preached came straight from the mind of God.

Demonstrating the coherence of the divine mind was one of the fathers' major preoccupations. The Bible, which was the written vehicle by which that mind could be known, therefore had to be coherent, despite its many authors, literary styles, and so on. Above all, it had to be shown that the Old Testament is not alien to the New. The fact that many of its provisions had lapsed with the coming of Christ was to be explained by saying that they were redundant, not that they were (or had been) wrong. The need to do this consistently led inevitably to a spiritual interpretation of the Old Testament text that did not cancel it out but rather revealed its true meaning.

### Law and Gospel

The contrast between the law and the gospel is familiar to Protestant Christians because of Martin Luther's famous repudiation of the former in his proclamation of the latter. But neither Luther nor the fathers of the church understood this contrast in quite the way in which many modern interpreters do. For them, law was basically a good thing because it proclaimed the order that there is in the universe. Paganism did not have any equivalent to that—the world of pagan deities was chaotic and unpredictable. Nobody really knew how to make fortune smile on them, though all sorts of options were tried at one time or another.

From the biblical standpoint, the law of the Lord was perfect, reviving the soul (Ps 19:7). The apostle Paul said that it was holy, a true expression of the mind of God (Rom 7:12). The problem he faced was not the law but our inability to keep it. The law could diagnose what is wrong with us but could not do anything to put it right. Pagans also had a high regard for law and often saw their classical lawgivers as divinely inspired in some way. But pagan laws were the products of tradition, hallowed by centuries of practice and often unchangeable. To go against the law was to disturb the social order and invite chaos. The results could be catastrophic. The classic case of failure was the condemnation of Socrates, who was forced to commit suicide because he had supposedly defamed the gods of Athens. There was no way out of that. Punishment was an inexorable fate that could be neither avoided nor deflected.

The biblical view is completely different. In the Bible, law reveals the mind of God, but this mind is a living thing that can (and must) be applied according to circumstances, and there is always room for forgiveness and restoration. At the heart of God's law is his love, and at the heart of his love is grace and mercy. There is no question of denying the law or of watering it down in any way—justice must be done, and justice involves punishment and destruction. But instead of annihilating the guilty, Christian judgment sees the sinless Son of God taking the punishment on himself, thereby setting sinners free from the obligation to self-destruct. There is no inexorable law, no fate that cannot be avoided.

Completely missing from any pagan scheme of moral or spiritual improvement is the notion of deliverance for those who are unworthy of it. The salvation of the undeserving goes completely against the mindset of the pagan world, but it is the essence of the gospel. Pagans prided themselves on their mental and physical superiority to others—philosophers because of their superior intellects, athletes because of their physical prowess. Statues of their great men often portrayed them as naked and unashamed, because the perfection of their bodies spoke for the purity of their souls. Christians could not accept that. There is no such thing as a perfect Christian, because all have sinned and fallen short of the glory of God. No amount of human effort can bring anyone closer to heaven—that is the gift of God alone. Many people confuse predestination with fate, but in fact the two are complete opposites. Christian predestination focuses on the salvation of the unworthy, but pagan fatalism was more usually directed to the destruction of the worthy. Its symbol was not the broken body of Christ but the Achilles heel—the flaw in perfection that led to death, not to eternal life.

The Christian understanding of perfect good had a direct impact on the way that the church fathers interpreted the Bible. At one level the Bible contained precepts that were meant to be applied in this life. This was how the Jews read the Old Testament, and within the limits of their understanding they were right to do so. Where they erred was in thinking that by keeping the law in this way they were pleasing God. But God is perfect and cannot be reduced to the parameters of this world, where perfection is impossible. What was required was a spiritual rebirth, and that could be had only in and through Jesus Christ. To become a Christian was to acquire his mind and be exposed to a different mental and spiritual universe. This dimension of reality was also revealed in the Bible, but often in ways that concealed it from those who did not possess the necessary understanding. Christian interpretation of Scripture had to go beyond the surface and penetrate the deeper meaning of the text, which was possible only with the help of the indwelling presence of the Holy Spirit speaking to the heart. This is clearly stated in the New Testament, and it provides the key to the correct reading of the sacred texts as a whole. Jews and gentiles came at this from different starting points, but both needed the spiritual transformation that only Christ could offer. Once that had taken place, the things that had divided them in their previous lives fell away, and they were united in a new hermeneutic centered on and illuminated by the gospel of God's eternal salvation.

SUMMARY

We can now summarize our findings as follows:

1. Christians and Jews both regarded the Hebrew Scriptures as divinely inspired, but they interpreted them very differently. For Christians, the key to understanding them lay in the life, death, and resurrection of Jesus the Messiah. The Jews rejected this and continued to read the text as an exposition of the law of Moses that had to be applied to every aspect of life. This led to the development of the rabbinical tradition which could not be reconciled with a Messianic reading of the texts.

2.  Christians claimed that the Hebrew Bible was a revelation of eternal truths that pagan philosophers had tried to discover on their own. They believed that Plato had read the laws of Moses and tried to apply them to his own culture, but without understanding them, because he did not know the God who had revealed them to his people. As a result, pagan societies suffered a disconnect between reason and religion which made it impossible for them to put the truth into practice, even if they knew what it was. Christianity reconciled theory with practice and was therefore the answer to the problems that the leading pagan thinkers had been trying to solve.

3.  The church fathers wanted to teach the basic principles of monothesim, creation, theodicy, and eschatology. There is only one God who is different from the world which he has created and which he governs according to his rational will. Evil (the problem of theodicy) is not inherent in matter or in the created order but is a rebellion of rational creatures—angels and human beings—against the will of God. Above all, the world has a purpose that will be fulfilled at the end of time, when injustice will be overcome and those who know God will be saved to live in eternity with him.

4.  The church fathers had to speak to pagans in language that they would understand but were determined not to be trapped by that into corrupting their message. They borrowed the concepts of philosophy but inverted them by proclaiming that those concepts had to be understood as aspects of revealed truth, not as conclusions drawn from human speculation.

# III

## THE FOUR SENSES
### of INTERPRETATION

### DEVELOPMENT OF THE SENSES

**T**he first systematic Christian interpreter of Scripture was Clement of Alexandria, who was influenced by Platonism as this had developed in the Greco-Roman world of his time. Particularly significant for him were the commentaries on the Torah (Pentateuch) written by the Jewish scholar Philo of Alexandria (c. 20 BC–AD 50), who had been a contemporary of Jesus and Paul. Like Justin Martyr, Philo believed that all truth is one and that it was revealed above all in the Torah. Greek philosophers like Plato were as close to the truth as they were because they had read the Torah and adapted it for their own purposes. Given that the Torah was already in existence when Plato was alive, Philo's belief was not totally impossible, but there is no evidence for his claim and we must conclude that it was wishful thinking on his part. As modern scholars have realized, what Philo was really doing was adapting the teachings of the Torah to the norms of Greek philosophy. Pagan Alexandrians had already done this with Homer, who had an iconic status in the Greek world similar to that of Moses among the Jews, and Philo employed much the same techniques in his reading of the Hebrew Bible. What this amounted to was an acceptance that the text could not be taken literally but had to be read in a figurative, or allegorical, manner. Stories about the creation and the fall were not historical accounts of what happened but picture images of a profound spiritual truth that could best be conveyed in story form. On that basis, Philo argued that the Torah gives a better and more coherent explanation of reality than anything produced by the Greeks. The reason for that was simple—as Philo saw it, the Bible is a revelation from the Creator, whereas Greek thought is just the imagination of the philosophers in question. Both traditions claimed to be rational, but Greek reason was contoured to fit the relativity of human existence whereas biblical reason went beyond that to sound out the mind of God. If that appeared to some Greeks to be irrational, it was because they did not have access to that higher knowledge—God had not revealed himself to them and so they lacked the key needed for understanding.

Clement took up this approach but went beyond Philo because he focused everything on the historical revelation of God in Christ. What for Philo had remained a relatively abstract interpretation of the Old Testament in allegorical terms was for Clement a revelation that found its fulfillment in the life, death, and resurrection of Jesus. Clement regarded the Hebrew Bible as the speech of the divine Word (*Logos*), who was Christ, speaking about himself.[1] This belief ensured that every word of the Old Testament had special significance as a revelation *of* God as well as *from* him, even if it was hard to understand. Clement went even further than this. He claimed that

---

1. Clement of Alexandria, *Exhortation to the Greeks* 9.82, 84.

the Lord had deliberately spoken about himself in a mysterious way because he did not want everyone to understand him—at least not immediately or without special training.[2] He supported this claim by saying that Jesus taught in parables, which he regarded as a form of allegory that was not intended to be immediately clear to the listener.[3] Admittedly, not all of Scripture was enigmatic, and there were plenty of passages that could be understood by everyone, including those who were unenlightened by the Holy Spirit. But the goal of the Christian life was to move on to higher things, and that meant learning the hermeneutic of allegorical interpretation, which alone revealed the theological meaning of the biblical text.[4]

Clement was aware that allegory could easily degenerate into fantasy, as it had with the various Gnostic interpretations that he was forced to combat. He insisted that the literal meaning of the biblical text had to be preserved, and that any figurative interpretation had to conform to what was fitting for God and consonant with other passages of Scripture.[5] But that did not prevent him from speculating about the Torah in ways that manifest an obvious debt to Philo. For example, Clement portrays Abraham as the symbol of faith, with his wife Sarah as wisdom and his concubine Hagar as pagan culture.[6] In typical Philonic fashion, Clement says that the fact that Hagar gave birth to a son before Sarah did was a revelation of the preparatory role that pagan Greek learning had in opening up the way for true wisdom to bear its fruit (in Isaac).[7] Elsewhere, he interprets the

---

2. Clement of Alexandria, *Miscellanies* 1.9.45

3. Clement of Alexandria, *Miscellanies* 6.15.124. Cf. Matt 13:34.

4. Clement of Alexandria, *Miscellanies* 1.28.176, 179.

5. Clement of Alexandria, *Miscellanies* 7.16.96.

6. The apostle Paul allegorized Sarah and Hagar, of course, so the idea was not new to Clement, though his application was different. See Gal 4:21, 31.

7. Clement of Alexandria, *Miscellanies* 1.3.30–31.

Ten Commandments as symbolic of the ten elements of which the world was believed to consist: sun, moon, stars, clouds, light, wind, water, air, darkness, and fire.[8] This is obviously far-fetched, as we can see when we try to correlate the elements with the actual commandments. Are we supposed to believe that the Sabbath day would always be cloudy? What has fire to do with the prohibition against covetousness? The absence of any connection, clear or hidden, was bound to bring this kind of interpretation into question, and it must be said that the fathers of a later time were much more restrained in their speculations than Clement sometimes was.

Clement of Alexandria did not expound his hermeneutic in a systematic way, but his pupil Origen developed an interpretative scheme that would become foundational for all subsequent patristic exegesis. Not all the fathers followed Origen in detail and in later centuries his approach came under increasing strain as its inadequacies were exposed, but whether subsequent commentators copied him or not, they all had to come to terms with his legacy. We must therefore consider what that legacy was and examine how it shaped the developing mind of the church.

In essentials, Origen followed Clement's lead, particularly in the latter's identification of the Bible with Christ as the Word of God and the implications which that identification had for his interpretation of the text. But whereas Clement tended to be discursive and rambling, mentioning particular principles as they occurred to him without developing them in detail, Origen organized his material in a systematic and comprehensive way. He did not concentrate on just a few biblical books, as those who wrote before him usually did, but extended his research to the whole of the Bible. He was the first Christian to comment on such relatively neglected writings as Joshua and Judges,

---

8. Clement of Alexandria, *Miscellanies* 6.16.33.

as well as Job and Ecclesiastes. Furthermore, Origen developed his biblical studies along three distinct lines, which were to prove foundational for the future. The first and most basic of these was his determination to establish the correct text of the Scriptures, a concern that led him to do research into the Hebrew originals of the Old Testament. The second was his devotion to extended commentary, in which he expounded the meaning of particular passages, often at considerable length. Finally, he was a preacher who applied his findings to the lives of ordinary Christian people, most of whom had no theological training of any kind. This combination—exegesis, exposition, and application—established a pattern that would last for centuries and was followed by John Calvin (1509–1564), who in many ways laid the foundation for modern biblical studies.

Origen was the first Christian to write a hermeneutical treatise, *First Principles* (*Peri archōn* in Greek or *De principiis* in Latin), which allows us to speak with assurance about his overall method and approach. Origen believed that the Bible speaks to the whole person, who is a composite of body, soul, and spirit. Starting from that assumption, he argued that there are three senses of interpretation, corresponding to this tripartite human nature. Later on, a fourth sense would be added, which spoke about the glorified life in heaven. Origen interpreted that as belonging to the spiritual dimension of the human being and never took matters any further, though there are several examples in his writings of what would later be distinguished as the fourth sense.[9]

At the same time, Origen connected the three dimensions of the biblical text to three types of readers, each of whom were able to approach the Bible at their own level. First of all there were the beginners (*incipientes*), who studied the bodily sense of the text more than

---

9. See Origen, *First Principles* 4.1–3, where he lists a number of earthly phenomena (Jerusalem, Israel, etc.) and explains that they are pictures of heavenly realities.

anything else. Then there were the more advanced learners (*progredientes*) who had moved on from there to consider its moral implications. Finally, there were the achievers (*perfecti*) who had mastered the techniques of interpretation and were able to appreciate the full spiritual depth of God's revelation.[10] The Bible has something to say to everyone, and it was Origen's self-appointed task to clarify what that was in each individual case.

It is tempting to say that Origen made a basic distinction between the literal and the higher senses of interpretation, which included both the soul and the spirit, but this is misleading. There were certainly times when he thought that the literal sense had its own integrity but that it was of little use to the church. He did not invent this idea but took it straight from the apostle Paul, who interpreted Deuteronomy 25:4, about not muzzling the ox who treads out the corn, as applying to the need for the church to support its pastors and teachers (1 Cor 9:9–10).[11] In a similar vein, Origen interpreted the detailed instructions given to the Old Testament priests about preparing the burnt offerings as literally true but useless for the needs of the church. The priest who tore away the outer skin of the sacrificial animal was to be compared to the teacher who removes the outer covering, or "letter," of the word of God to reveal the spiritual understanding that constitutes its inner parts.[12]

In addition to that, there are many scriptural passages in which the "literal" sense does not apply to the human body but speaks directly to the soul or the spirit. The prime example of this is the Song of Songs, which for Origen had no bodily application at all. This is not because he had an aversion to human sexuality but because

---

10. Origen wrote in Greek, of course, but the surviving texts are in Latin, which explains the Latin terminology used here.

11. Origen, *First Principles* 4.2.6.

12. Origen, *Homilies on Leviticus* 1.4, 5.1.

he saw no connection between that and the text of the Song.[13] Of course, he recognized that the Song appears to be an epithalamium (a poem in celebration of a marriage), but when compared to other works of that genre, it comes across as disjointed and inconsistent. The Song does not progress from courtship to marriage, and there is no union of the bridegroom with his bride. The sensuality of the poem is not an end in itself but points the way to higher things that remain beyond the grasp of those who are bound to this world. For Origen, the conclusion was obvious—the spirit of the Song leads the reader away from an attachment to worldly things and points the reader toward the need for a spiritual transformation that cannot be realized in time and space.

Once this principle is accepted, the reader of the Song will come to see that it is the hermeneutical key to interpreting the entire Bible.[14] Beginning with the six days of creation, God has revealed a pattern of spiritual principles that are embedded in material being and made accessible to rational creatures, but that cannot be reduced to their level. On the contrary, the principles are placed there in order to stimulate human beings, who are both material and rational, to seek the mind of the God who has made us and to draw nearer to him.

Having examined the development of the senses of interpretation, we can now look at the individual senses in more depth.

## THE BODILY SENSE

We must begin with the bodily sense because that is where the first readers of the text started. It is the most obvious of Origen's three senses and may even be dominant in the historical books of

---

13. See J. Christopher King, *Origen on the Song of Songs as the Spirit of Scripture: The Bridegroom's Perfect Marriage-Song* (Oxford: Oxford University Press, 2005), 54.

14. King, *Origen on the Song of Songs*, 148.

the Bible. The church fathers saw little need to write commentaries on the Old Testament books of Samuel and Kings, for example, and even the Acts of the Apostles was not expounded in detail until the fourth century and later. This was not because the books were rejected as Scripture but because their meaning was thought to be too obvious to need further explanation. The same was true for passages that give clear moral instruction, like much of the Ten Commandments, the Sermon on the Mount, and 1 Corinthians 13. It seems strange to modern readers that some of the best-known parts of the Bible were often passed over by ancient commentators, but when we realize that nobody was expected to be puzzled by them or find them problematic, we can see why they were relatively neglected.

The bodily sense was often present in other parts of the Bible, where it served to conceal a deeper meaning, though this did not make it inapplicable as it stood. The Jewish food laws, for example, were followed closely even by many Jewish Christians, and there was nothing wrong with that as long as nobody thought that observing them brought a believer closer to God. Origen even suggested that the bodily sense acts as a preservative by protecting the deeper senses and keeping them ready for those with spiritual perception to find them, as Jewish believers in Christ eventually did. For the most part, though, the bodily sense served to condemn the reader by convicting him of sin. This had been clearly intimated in Paul's exposition of the law in Romans 7, and to that extent it served as a valuable preparation for the gospel. If the impossible demands of the law drove people to seek salvation in Christ, then so much the better.

The main fact about the bodily sense, though, is that, like our human bodies, it is confined to time and space. In the resurrection, and especially after the return of Christ and the consummation of all things, it will have no further purpose and will disappear. This does not mean that students of Scripture should ignore the bodily sense, but rather that they should bear in mind that it is not the ultimate purpose of God's revelation. True believers must seek to go beyond it wherever possible and not be misled into thinking that following it is all that they need to do to know Christ.

## THE MORAL SENSE

The second sense, connected with the human soul, is usually called "moral," but this is because we lack a suitable word for it. It could perhaps be called "psychic," but that word has other connotations in English that make it difficult to use in this context without misunderstanding.[15] This is a pity, because the moral or psychic sense is key to understanding Origen's overall approach to biblical interpretation. For him, it is the first step on the road to salvation because it takes us from the material world into the higher realm of the spirit. At the same time, it keeps us tied to material existence in a way that the purely spiritual sense does not, and therefore serves as a kind of bridge between the sensual and the spiritual realms. Its primary importance lies in its accessibility. The Jews who received the Old Testament revelation did not need to be told about Christ in order to understand that it was wrong for them to kill, commit adultery, or steal. But, as Paul pointed out to the Romans, the moral sense of the Bible was a constant challenge to its readers because it made them aware of their sinfulness and served as a constant rebuke to their baser desires. Direct personal engagement with the demands of the law was necessary for spiritual growth to take place, and believers were expected to prepare themselves in order to receive the higher truths concealed within and beyond it.

---

15. It is, however, the term of choice for Elizabeth Ann Dively Lauro, *The Soul and Spirit of Scripture within Origen's Exegesis* (Leiden: Brill, 2005).

Christians need to pay attention to the moral sense of Scripture because if we do not grow in virtue, we shall never see Christ. If our minds are distracted by the sins of this life and we show no hunger or thirst for righteousness, we shall never be filled with it. Modern Christians may be tempted to see this as a form of salvation by works, but that is mistaken. Origen did not believe that the moral sense was a substitute for the gospel for the simple reason that it is confined to this life. It is a call to act in this world in a way that is pleasing to God, something that allows us to hope for a higher truth without being that truth itself. Its importance lies in the fact that if we do not prepare ourselves in this way, the higher truth will never be made known to us because the spiritual realm will be unable to connect with our material existence.

The significance of this was most obvious among Jewish believers before the coming of Christ. They were waiting for the appearance of the Messiah and preparing for that great day by following the Law and the Prophets as much as they could. They recognized that the Old Testament held out the promise of his coming, and as time went on, they grew ever more eager for it to be fulfilled. This is how Origen interpreted the way in which the Jews understood the Song of Songs. The Song opens with the statement that he (the bridegroom) kissed me (the bride) with the kisses of his mouth, but before the coming of Christ this remained an aspiration rather than an actual experience. The Jews waited for the bridegroom to come and kiss them with the words of his mouth. The Song was a constant reminder of what to expect, and when he finally arrived, their passionate longing was satisfied. Had they not been so disposed to begin with, though, the bridegroom would have come and found them asleep, like the foolish virgins in the parable of Jesus, and they would have missed out on his blessing.

## THE SPIRITUAL SENSE

To Origen's way of thinking, the core of the Bible is the spiritual sense, which is only accessible to those who have the mind of Christ. For that reason it was closed to the Jews, who could never penetrate its depths. They were doomed to be frustrated in their attempts to substitute the moral sense of the law for the presence of God in their midst. The spiritual sense is not only a revelation but also a participation in the wisdom of God. It is meaningful only to those whose lives have been transformed, who have been born again. It can be experienced in this life, but its focus is on eternity, not on time and space. Jesus Christ is its theme, and the spiritual sense reveals his presence throughout the Bible, especially in the Old Testament where it is otherwise carefully hidden. It is those who are spiritual who constitute the church of the living God, the body of Christ, and the chosen ones who will share his victory over the forces of sin and death at the end of time.

This is a mystery that is in some respects unfathomable, though Origen was not above speculating about it when he got the chance. For example, he believed that the 144,000 whose foreheads bear the names of God and the Lamb (Rev 7:3–4; 14:1–5) represent an elite group of believers who are distinguished from the rest of us because they are biblical scholars who have devoted their lives to the study of the sacred text![16] That Origen himself was one of this chosen band goes without saying, but this should not be seen as evidence of inordinate human pride. As far as he was concerned, to know Christ is to know his mind, and his mind is revealed in Scripture. Therefore, the appearance of extraordinary zeal for studying the word of God is evidence of a deep desire to be more like Christ—a desire that

---

16. Peter W. Martens, *Origen and Scripture: The Contours of the Exegetical Life* (Oxford: Oxford University Press, 2012), 90–91.

God is sure to reward. Modern readers may be disinclined to limit the number of such people to a mere 144,000, but the church is much larger today than it was in Origen's time. His interpretation may strike us as odd, but the message behind it is surely one with which all Christians will agree: Christ cannot be separated from the Bible, and to know one is to hunger and thirst after a deeper knowledge of the other. Furthermore, we believe that those who seek will find what they are looking for and be rewarded by experiencing the presence of God in their lives. In that way, what Origen said strikes a chord with us today and we can affirm his basic belief, even if we would express it somewhat differently and not be as closely tied to the literal reading of apocalyptic prophecy as he was.

### THE HARMONY OF THE THREE SENSES

Just as the body, soul, and spirit of a living human being work together, so the three senses of biblical interpretation operate in harmony with one another. This theme comes across most clearly in the way that Origen treated the story of Noah's ark.[17] At the bodily level, he defended the historicity of Noah and the flood, going to great lengths to explain how so many animals could live together for forty days in such a confined space.[18] This line of argument was no more persuasive in his time than it is in ours, but he insisted on it because it was important for him to stress that God's justice and mercy are historically verifiable realities and not just theoretical concepts.

After making that point, Origen goes directly to the spiritual sense, linking the flood to the last judgment and the ark to the church, which alone is capable of saving us from the wrath to come. Origen did not invent this parallel—it can be found in the teaching of Jesus

---

17. See Dively Lauro, *Soul and Spirit of Scripture*, 132–47.

18. Origen, *Homily on Genesis* 2.1.

(Matt 24:37–39; Luke 17:26–27) and also in that of the apostle Peter (1 Pet 3:18–20), where the flood waters are compared to the water of baptism. The parallels are not exact, but they were good enough for Origen, who did not hesitate to equate the three decks of the ark mentioned in Genesis 6:16 with the three senses of interpretation. He even relied on the translation of an obscure Hebrew word as "square planks" to make the astounding assertion that these planks were "the teachers in the Church, the leaders, and zealots of the faith" who stand fast against the assaults of enemies without and heretics within the body of Christ.[19]

Even more fanciful is the way that he apportions the rooms in the ark to different kinds of people and animals. On the top deck are the intimates of Jesus who, like the family of Noah, are few in number. The lower decks house a multitude of irrational animals and savage beasts who have not been tamed by the power of faith. But some are less savage than others, and they occupy the middle deck, closer to the charmed circle at the top.[20] It is clear that Origen has let his imagination run away with him, but the basic idea that the church contains people at many levels of spiritual progress and that all are saved, regardless of how close to God they have come, is something that modern minds can accept, even if the connection to Noah's ark seems far-fetched.

What we are dealing with here is a presumed link between two separate realities that is nonexistent in actual fact. We may compare Origen's hermeneutic to astrology. Astrology is the belief that the stars hold the key to understanding the fate of human beings, and many people have taken this seriously. A good astrologer had to become a skilled astronomer in order to have the clues needed to

---

19. Origen, *Homily on Genesis* 2.4.
20. Origen, *Homily on Genesis* 2.3.

decipher the mysteries of human life, and astronomy is a recognized science. Similarly, the good astrologer had to be a gifted psychologist, able to read the minds of those who sought his knowledge and to advise them sensibly. Psychology of that kind is less scientific, but it is a gift that some people possess, and they can be quite prescient when it comes to working out what is likely to happen to certain individuals. The problem is that there is no connection between the two things other than the one that the astrologer has concocted in his own mind. Origen's spiritual interpretation of Noah's ark is similar to this. He takes the physical details recorded in Genesis 6 and regards them as real, and then looks at the church, with its different kinds of members. His separate analysis of both things has a certain integrity, but there is no real link between them, and so his interpretation must be regarded as fanciful.

This makes it very difficult to decide what value Origen's hermeneutic might possess. In strictly objective terms it is wrong, and some scholars have not hesitated to reject it for that reason.[21] But although that is true, is it missing the point? Origen's primary concern was to preach a valid spiritual message to the church. A strictly literal account of Noah and the flood might have some interest to antiquarians, but it would do nothing to influence the spiritual condition of Christian believers. From Origen's point of view it was better to use the ark as a picture image for a church that people could recognize and to explain its internal variety and spiritual condition in a way that made sense to them. Noah's ark was a potentially useful illustration of this, even if the way Origen used it can hardly be called a serious hermeneutic.

The matter is complicated still further by the way in which Origen treats the moral sense that he finds in Noah's ark. As he put it, "If

---

21. As, for example, R. P. C. Hanson, *Allegory and Event* (London: SCM, 1959).

there is anyone who, while evils are increasing and vices are overflowing, can turn from the things which are in flux, passing away and fallen, and can hear the Word of God and the heavenly precepts, this man is building an ark of salvation within his own heart."[22] There is no attempt to make any connection with the historical ark or with the church, but only a direct application to the heart and mind of the individual believer. Christians are surrounded by a flood of evil in the world and have to protect themselves against it. By clinging to the word of God, they can rise above the flood, in effect creating a kind of "ark" that will protect them from it and lead in the end to eternal salvation. It is good practical advice and makes a specific demand of the hearers, who are required not merely to contemplate the many-colored reality of the church but to do something to advance their own spiritual condition. Modern readers can relate to this because the need to fortify ourselves against the overwhelming temptations of the present age is as great now as it ever was. We may reject Origen's hermeneutic and dismiss the connection to Noah's ark, but the spiritual counsel that he gave in his sermon is as valid and as uplifting today as it was then. When reading the exegesis of the fathers, therefore, we must learn to separate the wheat from the chaff and find a more solid scriptural basis on which to ground our teaching. Origen and the fathers who followed his lead may have misinterpreted their texts and indulged in fanciful comparisons that fail to meet the standards of interpretation that we would now expect, but there is usually a kernel—and often much more than that—of truth in what they have to say, and if that kernel can be rescued and recycled, it is worth doing. In the presence of God we stand together—one in the Spirit, even when we interpret that oneness in very different ways.

---

22. Origen, *Homily on Genesis* 2.6.

The fourth sense of interpretation was developed by John Cassian (c. 360–435) and is generally known today as "anagogical."[23] It does not depend on an analysis of the human body but refers to the transposed state in which believers will flourish after they rise from the dead and go to be with Christ in heaven. It was not distinguished as a separate sense of interpretation in the patristic period, but many of its basic ingredients can be found in the fathers' writings, particularly in Origen. It is therefore best to say that John Cassian did not invent a fourth sense of interpretation but redefined the existing three by splitting the spiritual sense into two—one concerned with this life and the other with the next. In that form the different senses of biblical interpretation were to pass into the Middle Ages and become standard everywhere in Western Europe.

The most frequent comparison they made was between Jerusalem and the city of God in heaven, already defined in Revelation 21:10–14 but present elsewhere in Scripture as well—for example, in Galatians 4:25–26 and perhaps also in Ezekiel 40–48, with its detailed description of the eschatological temple.

Once this parallel is accepted, virtually every reference to Jerusalem (or to Mount Zion, which is often regarded as a synonym for the Holy City) that can be found anywhere in the Bible, but especially in the Psalms, can be interpreted in an anagogical fashion, and was. The poetic nature of the Psalms gives this approach a certain validity, since it is clear that Jerusalem/Zion represents the people of God in some way and that references to it/them are not historical but prophetic. To that extent, at least, the anagogical sense of Scripture is more solidly grounded than either the moral or the spiritual ones are, and traces of it can still be found in serious commentary writing today.

---

23. John Cassian, *Conferences* 14.8.

We can now summarize our findings as follows:

1. The early Christians believed that the Hebrew Bible and the apostolic writings—which by AD 200 they were treating as a New Testament—were a coherent message of salvation revealing the mind of the Creator and Redeemer God. This approach can be seen in the writings of second century theologians like Irenaeus and Tertullian, but it reached its most systematic form in the teaching of Origen, the most prolific and profound interpreter of the Bible in ancient times.

2. Origen believed that the Bible had three different senses, or levels of interpretation, corresponding to the body, soul, and spirit of the human being. There were two reasons for this. One was that the word of God speaks to the whole person, and not simply to the mind. The other was that it was a manual of instruction that addressed itself to beginners, more advanced learners, and those who had attained spiritual perfection. It was impossible to grow out of the Bible, because as one advanced in faith and knowledge, one's understanding of the text's meaning grew deeper and more comprehensive.

3. Origen believed that the bodily sense spoke to the condition of the fallen human race and showed how inadequate purely human resources are in the effort to attain perfection. The moral sense of the Bible was given in order to challenge the soul to seek higher things, but it too failed in the end, because although it held out a vision of what was required it could not provide the

means by which the seeker after truth could attain to it. The spiritual sense was necessary for that, but it was only revealed to those who had the Spirit of Christ dwelling in their hearts by faith.

4. In the fourth century John Cassian and others developed a fourth sense of interpretation by dividing the spiritual sense into two parts, one which applies to life in this world and the other which speaks about eternal life in heaven. Much of what the Bible says about Jerusalem as the City of God, and many of the Psalms, came to be interpreted in this sense.

5. The four senses of interpretation encouraged metaphorical readings of the biblical text, and especially of the Old Testament. Some of these interpretations respected the historical context of the original text and applied it to a spiritual understanding by way of what we call typology. But other interpretations ignored the original sense of the text and spiritualized it completely as allegory. Origen was a particularly enthusiastic user of allegory, as can be seen from the way he understood the story of Noah.

# IV

## THE SEARCH for CONSENSUS

### THE FLIGHT FROM ALLEGORY

The hermeneutical achievement of Origen set the agenda for the rest of the patristic period and beyond, but important though it was, it did not dominate the field entirely. There was not much development for a generation or two after Origen's death, but after Christianity was legalized in 312, things began to change. Not only did it become possible for Christians to preach, teach, and write freely, but they had to equip a blossoming church with a full range of tools for understanding their sacred texts and applying them to everyday life. Not surprisingly, therefore, homilies, commentaries, and theological textbooks of different kinds made their appearance, as did liturgies for use in public worship. Biblical interpretation was no longer an academic exercise practiced by a scholarly elite but an everyday concern that affected Christians at every level.

It was at this time that the New Testament finally came into its own as Scripture in the fullest sense of the word. Its books were already known and used as the word of God, though there were some doubts about which books should be regarded as divinely inspired and whether they should be read in the same way as the Hebrew Bible. The main reason for that was the different way in which the New Testament treated its subject matter. All Christians agreed that the Bible spoke primarily about Jesus Christ, but whereas the Old Testament did this in many ways, as the writer to the Hebrews put it (Heb 1:1), which were obscured by prophetic language that was hard for the casual reader to interpret, the New Testament spoke about what had already happened. The Gospels might contain parables and promises of future fulfillment, but most of what they said about Christ was straightforwardly historical. The word spoken to the prophets had been accomplished in real time, and the gospel writers did little more than record the facts. Similarly, the apostolic Epistles were for the most part perfectly clear instructions given to particular churches and could be readily understood.

The great exception to this general rule was the book of Revelation, but it is instructive to note that for that very reason Revelation was often set aside and even rejected by some. That it was almost entirely symbolic and allegorical was clear to everybody, but whether such a text had a place in the New Testament was not universally agreed. Somewhat oddly, the Western (Latin-speaking) churches tended to accept it as Scripture, whereas the Eastern (mainly Greek-speaking) churches were more reluctant, and even today the lectionaries of the Eastern Orthodox churches generally omit it. Why this should have been so is not clear, given that the Romans were generally thought to be more pragmatic and the Greeks more inclined to mysticism, but that generalization is clearly inadequate in this case. The book of Revelation is one of the glories of Greek literature and continues to exercise its peculiar fascination to the present day, but the truth is that it was not immediately appreciated by the Greeks as God's word. It was one thing for the Old Testament to be a theological puzzle, fully decipherable only by allegory, but in the New Testament the veil that had lain over the face of Moses had been taken away and there seemed to be no valid reason for trying to put it back again, albeit in a different place (2 Cor 3:13).

The overall effect of this attitude led to a growing reluctance to rely on allegorical interpretation as the key to understanding the Scriptures, even though its usefulness was recognized in certain situations and it was never abandoned completely. But the willingness of Origen to look for hidden meanings even in the plain teachings of Jesus and the apostles was no longer so evident, and critical voices could increasingly be heard. In the most famous case, Jerome, the great translator of the Bible into Latin, went from being an admirer of Origen to becoming one of his fiercest critics, but his dramatic change was exceptional. Most people were more moderate in their reactions, disputing particular interpretations put forward by Origen without rejecting his approach completely.

An example of that can be found in the writings of Eustathius of Antioch (d. c. 360), who criticized Origen for allegorizing the story of King Saul and the witch of Endor (1 Sam 28:1–25), which he thought made perfect sense as it stood and did not require such treatment.[1] This approach was supported, and may even have been inspired, by the works of Eusebius of Caesarea (c. 265–340), who outlined the history of Israel on the basis of a literal reading of the Old Testament. Eusebius believed in the reality of typology and of biblical prophecy, but he was careful to restrict his interpretations to cases where the literal sense was unsatisfactory and he always referred his spiritual

---

1. Migne, PG 18, col. 656.

interpretations to the fulfillment of Old Testament prophecy in Christ. For example, he used the foundation stone that the Lord laid in Zion (Isa 28:14–17) as a type of Christ because any lesser interpretation seemed to him to be unworthy of the text. But even Eusebius could resort to allegory when he chose. In interpreting Isaiah 19:1 ("The LORD is riding on a swift cloud") he did not hesitate to say that the cloud stands for the human body assumed by the Logos in the incarnation of Christ.[2]

It is tempting to regard Eusebius's approach as a deliberate repudiation of Origen's hermeneutic, but that is going too far. As the above example shows, Eusebius was quite happy to use a spiritual interpretation when it suited the context, and poetic passages were particularly susceptible to it. He was particularly prone to do this with the Psalter, which he regarded as a digest of the entire Old Testament that was full of barely concealed references to Christ. Yet it is noticeable that he seldom ventured into allegory, except where well-established tradition encouraged him to do so, as in the way in which Babylon was used to stand for a world in opposition to God. That interpretation could be justified by an appeal to the book of Revelation, where Babylon is clearly used in that sense, though whether that was also the case in the Psalms may be doubted, even if many of the references to Jerusalem/Zion clearly point in that direction.

At times the disinclination to resort to spiritual interpretations could be taken to the opposite, and in many ways equally unsatisfactory, extreme. A case in point is the series of homilies on the six days of creation preached by Basil of Caesarea. Basil rejected the allegorical hermeneutic that went back to Origen and preferred what can only be called a scientific account of the events concerned. Most of what he says is a fascinating record of the biological and

---

2. Eusebius of Caesarea, *Extracts from the Prophets* 4.10.

zoological knowledge of his time, and in that respect Basil resembles the so-called six-day creationists of our own time. But we must admit that so literal an interpretation is just as improbable as Origen's and is almost certainly not what the original author had in mind.

Less extreme than Basil was his contemporary Diodore of Tarsus (d. 390), who rejected allegory in the pure sense and replaced it with what he termed *theōria*, which might be translated as "insight" and is closer to what we would now call typology. *Theōria* accepts the validity of the literal sense of a text but claims that it points to a higher spiritual meaning lying behind it. Thus, for example, Diodore accepted the historical accuracy of the story of Cain and Abel, but maintained that it signified the hostility of the Jews (as the elder brother) to the church.[3] At most this reading offers a parallel, not a prophecy of what was to come, and in that sense might be regarded as a sermon illustration not entirely without value, but it hardly counts as serious biblical interpretation. For the most part, Diodore stuck to the literal sense of the text, even in the Psalter, where he rejected Messianic interpretations unless they were accepted by Jews, a degree of deference to pre-Christian (and later on increasingly anti-Christian) sensibilities that was rare among the church fathers.

But the supreme example of flight from allegory is found in the commentaries of Diodore's pupil Theodore of Mopsuestia. In principle, Theodore was prepared to recognize the validity of typological interpretations of the Old Testament, such as that Jonah was a type of Christ, a view that can be found in the New Testament itself (Matt 12:38–42). But although he states that in the preface to his commentary on the book of Jonah, he does not follow through in the commentary itself, where no parallel with Christ is ever mentioned. This suggests that he paid lip service to a hermeneutic that was almost

---

3. Diodore of Tarsus, Corpus Christianorum: Series Graeca 6:7.

universally accepted but that he himself found uncongenial. It is certainly true that he avoided christological readings whenever he could and that, uniquely among the fathers, he regarded the Song of Songs as a human love story—and no more.

Theodore's reluctance to see Christ foreshadowed in the Old Testament probably derived from his theological understanding of human history. He believed that the world had gone through three phases of religious development, from a primitive polytheism to Judaic monotheism to Christian Trinitarianism. The first two were essentially human constructions. Pagans saw the divine in everything, whereas Jews saw it in nothing. Judaism was superior to paganism because it did not reduce God to the dimensions of time and space, but it went too far in the opposite direction. Christianity was a happy medium in that God is both transcendent and immanent in the person of Jesus Christ. His incarnation marked a new departure in our relationship to God, one in which the ultimate fulfillment of all things has become the overriding goal. As a result, instead of looking back to the Old Testament for types and figures of Christ, Theodore preferred to see the life of Christ as a prefiguration of the spiritual life of the Christian. Christ's baptism, for example, became for him the paradigm, or type, of our baptism as Christians. What he did during his time on earth is a picture of what his followers are meant to do in imitation of him. There is New Testament authority for saying this, because the apostle Paul told the Corinthians to be imitators of him, just as he was of Christ (1 Cor 11:1).

Theodore's approach represented a complete reworking of Origen's tripartite division based on body, soul, and spirit. In his mind, all three of these ran together. Baptism was a physical act applied to the body and directly linked to the physical baptism of Jesus by John the Baptist. It was also a moral challenge to live up to the high calling to ministry that it represented. Finally, it pointed the way to final regeneration and resurrection at the end of time. It was not necessary to resort to allegory or even to typology, because the reality was present in the life of the believer at all three levels of interpretation. It is not difficult to see from this why modern interpreters generally regard Theodore as the church father who is nearest to them in his way of thinking. Vestiges of ancient hermeneutical theory persist in his writings, of course—it would be surprising if they did not—but they appear to modern readers as minor blemishes that can be overlooked when the bigger picture is taken into consideration.

## RETREAT FROM FLIGHT

The drive to abandon as much allegory as possible did not drive all before it. Quite apart from the difficulty that even the most determined anti-allegorists had to shed the legacy of Origen, there were many who wanted to strike a balance. They recognized that Origen had overdone it and did not want to follow him all the way, but they also sensed an important truth in what he said. A revelation of a world beyond this one could not be expected to confine itself to words and terms relevant only to the time and space universe. Sooner or later, genuine spiritual experience would have to rise above the limitations of the created order, and if language meant for that order were to be used to describe it, some form of higher meaning would be inevitable. It was therefore entirely logical and to be expected that interpreters would seek to transcend the literal senses of their texts, even if they remained reluctant to go too far away from them.

A good example of this mediating tendency can be found in the commentaries of Gregory of Nyssa, the younger brother of Basil of Caesarea. Gregory wrote *On the Titles of the Psalms*, a comprehensive exposition of the Psalter in which he used the traditional five divisions (1–41, 42–72, 73–89, 90–106, 107–150) as stepping stones describing the progress of the convert from the time he repents until the time that he finally enters the joy of heaven. In the course of this work Gregory encounters a number of historical events but interprets them as so many challenges to raise our sights to a higher moral and spiritual vision. It is this intermediate level, the second of Origen's three senses of interpretation, that captured Gregory's imagination the most, and it is that which dominates his writing.

This pattern reaches its fruition in his *Life of Moses*, which he treated both historically and typologically, again within the broader framework of the escape from sin (Egypt) to the final consummation of all things (the entry into the promised land). Gregory never denied the historical accuracy of the biblical account, but saw in it parallels with the life of Christ and through him with the experience of the church. The crossing of the Red Sea is a type of baptism; the twelve springs of Exodus 15:27 are the twelve apostles; the manna that appeared in the desert is a symbol of the Logos, the bread of heaven on which we feed for our spiritual nourishment. Many of these types can be supported from the New Testament, so Gregory cannot be regarded as an innovator.[4] At most he was a theologian who systematized and extended what he found in the Gospels or in the Pauline Epistles and turned it into a fixed pattern of spiritual development. In this way, Gregory stuck closely to the Scriptures while at the same time harmonizing them in a spiritual hermeneutic that went beyond the letter of the text.

Gregory's mediating position can also be found in Theodoret of Cyrrhus, who was one of the most prolific commentators on the

---

4. Jesus referred to himself as the "bread of heaven" (John 6:32–34) and identified himself with the serpent that Moses had held up in the wilderness (John 3:14–15). The apostle Paul saw him as the rock that followed the people of Israel through the desert (1 Cor 10:4). In his own eyes, Gregory was doing no more than expounding the true meaning of the Torah.

Bible that the Greek-speaking world produced. Unlike Diodore of Tarsus and Theodore of Mopsuestia, Theodoret accepted the christological interpretation of the Old Testament, even to the point of regarding Isaac's blessing of Jacob (Gen 27:27–29) as referring to the coming of Christ. He did much the same thing with Moses's prayer in Exodus 17:11, despite the fact that there is no evidence to support it and the passage makes perfect sense as it stands. On the other hand, Theodoret avoided the extremes of christological interpretation in his commentary on the Psalter, limiting himself to those passages where the church already had a long tradition of reading the texts in the light of Christ. Needless to say, Theodoret rejected Theodore's literalistic interpretation of the Song of Songs and in many ways harkened back to Origen. But whereas Origen had read the Song consistently in the light of his tripartite analysis of the human being, Theodoret ignored that and concentrated on the spiritual sense only. The result is a simpler presentation, easier for the nonspecialist reader to absorb but somewhat bland when compared with his apparent model.

Another writer in a similar mold was Cyril of Alexandria, who filled his commentaries on the Old Testament with christological references, leaving the impression that he was one of Origen's most faithful disciples. Yet closer inspection will reveal that, in fact, Cyril paid most attention to the literal sense of the biblical text, which he often expounded to the neglect of any spiritual interpretation that it might have. For example, he accepted that Jonah was a type of Christ when he spent three days in the stomach of the great fish but did not extend the analogy to other aspects of Jonah's life. Neither Jonah's attempt to escape doing God's will nor his grief at the pardon God granted to Nineveh had any application to Christ, and Cyril rejected that suggestion. This reluctance to allegorize can be seen most clearly in his commentary on John's Gospel, which he interpreted almost exclusively in the literal sense, which he also did in his homilies on Luke.

This is understandable, given that the life of Jesus was the historical fulfillment of ancient prophecies and not yet another riddle to be resolved at the end of time, and Cyril was sensible enough to realize that parables were not the only (or even most important) form that Jesus' teaching took. Even so, it was hard for Cyril to escape allegory entirely. For example, when he discussed the miracle of the loaves and the fishes (John 6:9), he could not avoid saying that the five barley loaves represented the five books of the Torah, or that the fish stood for solid gospel preaching. It is a reminder to us that even the greatest patristic interpreters could not resist finding parallels between the Old and the New Testaments when they could, whether those parallels made sense or not.

One interesting result of the search for balance between allegorical and literal interpretations of the Bible was the gradual rehabilitation of the book of Revelation as canonical Scripture, though the effects of earlier skepticism were not easily overcome and no real consensus was reached. The first two Greek commentaries on the book appear only in the sixth or seventh centuries—precise dating is impossible—and they are attributed to Oecumenius of Tricca (Trikkala) and to Andrew of Caesarea in Cappadocia (Kayseri), respectively. Both commentaries are highly allegorical in character, but in a way that corresponds to the literal sense of the text itself. Having said that, Oecumenius was careful to avoid eschatological interpretations as much as possible and read the text in broader ecclesiastical terms. For him, the woman who gives birth in chapter 12 is Mary the mother of Jesus, and as far as we can tell, Oecumenius was the first person to suggest that. The harlot who sits on the throne is Rome, which Oecumenius contrasts with Constantinople, the new and Christian capital of the empire. As for the thousand-year reign of the saints, Oecumenius sees this as purely symbolic and refers it to the incarnation of Christ, without specifying an end date in the year AD 1000, which was still some centuries in the future.

Andrew of Caesarea, by contrast, tries to validate the book of Revelation by quotations in its favor taken from earlier fathers, including those who accepted a millenarian interpretation of it. He believed that the end of time was fast approaching, and so was more open than Oecumenius to the traditional millenarian viewpoint, though without specifying a determinate period of a thousand years. Even so, he interpreted the reign of the saints as lasting from the incarnation of Christ to the end of the world, which sets him apart from Oecumenius. Andrew also believed that the woman with the child was not Mary but the church, and regards the harlot on the throne as symbolic of secular rulers in general and not tied to Rome more than to anywhere else.

Differences of this kind are of interest to historians of millenarianism and of apocalyptic literature, but they are of little importance for patristic exegesis because the book of Revelation itself continued to be ignored by most of the Eastern church, at least for teaching purposes. Interpretations of its symbolism remained conjectural and so were of little use in the great christological controversies that preoccupied the Eastern churches from the fourth to the eighth centuries. By the time they were resolved, the habit of overlooking Revelation had taken hold and there was no figure comparable to Augustine in the West who could give it a meaning that would be generally accepted throughout the Eastern Christian world.

## THE LATIN WEST

When we turn from the Greek-speaking East to the Latin West, we find a broadly similar pattern of biblical interpretation, though with particular nuances that distinguish it. The most important single factor that made the Latin West different was the absence of an agreed biblical text until around AD 400. Before that, Latin writers either translated directly from the Greek or relied on unofficial translations that circulated in different places and that have been collected together in modern times as the so-called *Vetus Latina* (Old Latin) version(s). What surprises us today is the relative lack of concern that Latin writers showed for this difficult situation. They translated the Old Testament from the Greek Septuagint, which was already a translation, and seldom paid close attention even to the Greek. What mattered to them was the general sense of the text rather than the details, and although they sometimes admitted that a good knowledge of the original languages was desirable, they rarely tried to acquire it themselves. This is especially true of Augustine, who rewrote the history of the world on the basis of the Bible, but whose mastery of Greek was patchy.

This does not mean that what the Latin fathers had to say is of no value. The first of them, Tertullian, did not write biblical commentaries but showed a mastery of the text in his extensive opposition to Marcion's attempts to abandon the Old Testament and reduce the Gospels to an expurgated version of Luke. Tertullian was also attracted to the Montanists, an apocalyptic sect from Phrygia (in modern Turkey) that was especially influenced by a millenarian interpretation of the Johannine literature. The Montanists believed that the age of the Paraclete had arrived with their prophet Montanus and his assistants, and that the new Jerusalem mentioned in Revelation 21 would descend at a village called Pepuza in the year 177. That obviously did not happen, as Tertullian (writing at least twenty years later) must have known, but his fascination with the end of time was to characterize Western thought for some centuries after his time. Where escapades like those of the Montanists tended to make Easterners suspicious of the book of Revelation, its authority was never questioned in the West, even though Western writers recoiled from millenarianism just as much as their Eastern counterparts did.

This interest explains why commentaries on the book of Revelation can be found in the West to an extent that is not true of the East. The first one known to us was written by Victorinus of Pettau (d. c. 303), who exhibits much of the same ambivalence concerning allegory that would be found in the East later on. This is somewhat surprising given that even in its literal sense the book of Revelation is highly symbolic, and Victorinus did not hesitate to identify the woman in chapter 12 with the church and the beast in chapter 13 with the Roman Empire. Occasionally he went beyond such obvious identifications to more doubtful ones, as when he sees the eagle mentioned in Revelation 8:13 as representing the Holy Spirit. On the whole, however, Victorinus sticks to as literal an interpretation of the book as he can, especially with regard to the millennium and the new Jerusalem in Revelation 20. So alarmed was Jerome by this that a century later he issued a revised version of Victorinus's commentary, in which he took great care to spiritualize all such references!

In between Victorinus and Jerome came another commentary on Revelation, written by Tyconius (fl. c. 370–390), a Donatist who was also one of the most important writers on hermeneutics that the patristic era produced. Tyconius opted for a spiritual reading of the book, which he regarded as an allegory of the relationship between Christ and the church. His most important contribution to the ongoing interpretation of Revelation was the way in which he transcended the emphasis on a future fulfillment by reading the text as a commentary on the life of the church here and now. That effectively ruled out any millenarian reading, and it seems to have been this which appealed to both Jerome and Augustine, who valued his work highly even though they objected to his Donatism. More than a century later, Primasius of Hadrumetum (d. c. 560) wrote a commentary on Revelation in which he stated that he relied on both Augustine and Tyconius for its interpretation. That seems to have settled the matter, and for the next several centuries Primasius's synthesis, based largely on Tyconius, was the standard Western interpretation of the book. A series of early medieval commentators followed him more or less consistently, including Beatus of Liébana (730–800), to whom we owe the preservation of most of Tyconius's commentary.

Towering over biblical interpretation in the Latin West was Jerome, who moved the study of Scripture to an entirely new level. First of all, he understood that the Old Testament had to be translated from Hebrew, not from any Greek translation, and he set about doing that, despite his own rudimentary knowledge of the language. Getting to grips with the original text also brought Jerome face to face with the allegorizing tendencies of Origen, which he first accepted wholeheartedly and then rejected with just as much vehemence. This about-turn raised eyebrows in some quarters and strained friendships, particularly with Rufinus, who continued to value Origen and to translate his commentaries into Latin, but it helped to establish a permanent distinction between the work of the exegete and that of the theologian. In the Origenist view, the duty of the exegete was to find theology, even if allegory was the only way that could be done. But Jerome upheld the principle that not all Bible verses were meant to be a revelation of Christ or of the Trinity, and that in many cases a literal reading not only was to be preferred but was what God had intended when he inspired the sacred writers. Hiding the truth behind signs and figures was not the divine intention, nor did God want us to gloss over the seamier side of human life by finding spiritual interpretations for otherwise unpalatable utterances, like the writer's desire to kill the children of Babylon in Psalm 137.

Having said that, Jerome was not nearly as independent of Origen as he wanted to be. He fully accepted the tripartite senses of interpretation and applied them regularly, though by no means always consistently. Occasionally he even outdid Origen, as, for example, when he compared Jonah's flight to Tarshish to Christ's descent from heaven to "exile" on earth. He even stated that Jonah's sailing from the Palestinian port of Joppa (Jaffa) symbolized the fact that Christ started his earthly journey among the Jews, where his struggles got him into trouble (the storm at sea) and led to his death (the great fish). At the same time, Jerome insisted that not everything about Jonah was allegorical, though quite how he distinguished the literal from the typological is unclear. It seems that on many occasions it was more or less arbitrary, and that Jerome often swung from one extreme to the other for no apparent reason. What is true of his commentary on Jonah is also true of his expositions of the other prophets and of Matthew's Gospel, where his unacknowledged debt to Origen is painfully obvious much of the time. It is a reminder that even Origen's fiercest opponents could not escape his influence, which remained fundamental to patristic interpretation of the Bible throughout the ancient period.

Very different from Jerome, the exegete, was Augustine of Hippo, the theologian. In terms of technical expertise, Augustine could not hold a candle to Jerome, the linguist and skilled textual critic, but he was to be the one who would formulate and transmit enduring principles of hermeneutics to subsequent generations, at least in the West. It is one of the misfortunes of history that Augustine's writings were not translated into Greek until about 850 years after his death, by which time their influence, while not inconsiderable, was seen to be alien to the (by then) well-established Greek tradition. Augustine's hermeneutic is not above criticism, but its value is such that it is still widely read today. Conveniently for everyone, it is found in a single, fairly short book known to us as *Christian Instruction* (*De doctrina Christiana*). The title itself is suggestive of his whole approach to the subject. Nowadays, a book called *Christian Doctrine* would take the shape of a systematic theology, but for Augustine it was an essay in how to read and apply the teaching of the Bible, which for him was the church's only doctrine.

At the heart of Augustine's hermeneutic was his conviction that God is a God of love and that he has revealed himself to human beings in order to draw them closer to him. Because of that, almost any interpretation of a biblical text that furthers those ends can be accepted as genuine. This does not mean that Augustine was prepared to ignore the literal meaning, but that he felt free to develop it along spiritual or allegorical lines if that would help his hearers get closer to God. Most of his biblical exposition was in the form of sermons, of which only a small percentage—though still a considerable number—have survived. Because of this approach, it is difficult to classify Augustine in terms of the traditional categories of interpretation; he was neither a literalist nor an allegorist but a pastor who drew on the resources available to him as he felt the situation required. When dealing with Christian doctrine in the modern meaning of the term, he was content to stick to the literal sense of the text, particularly when interpreting the Pauline Epistles. In this he followed men like the anonymous Ambrosiaster, who were adept at reading the texts in the light of Roman law and Jewish customs. But when preaching on the Psalter, or on the Johannine literature, he did not hesitate to indulge in allegory if that served his purpose better. For example, when speaking of the precious ointment used to wipe the feet of Jesus at Bethany (John 12:3), Augustine pointed out that the word used to describe it was *pisticus* ("authentic, reliable"), related to Greek *pistis* ("faith"), which supposedly indicates that believers should anoint the feet of Jesus by the way they live out their faith.

In many ways, this kind of interpretation can be compared to what is often heard from pulpits today. Preachers are under pressure to relate their text to the practicalities of everyday life, and rhetorical flourishes like these, while indefensible in strictly hermeneutical terms, bring home an important message that the hearers can take away and apply to themselves. The technique seems to have been effective, though whether we should judge Augustine's exegesis by such criteria is more doubtful.

For that we need to look at writings where the interpretation of the text is primary and possible applications to the Christian life come later. We can do this best by looking at the way in which Augustine read the creation narratives in Genesis. We have already said that creation was a favorite theme of patristic exegetes, but Augustine outdid his peers by returning to the same theme time and time again. In his early days he was greatly taken with allegorical interpretations of Genesis, partly because he had been converted under the ministry of Ambrose of Milan, who was a staunch allegorist, but partly also because he thought it was the best way to counteract the charge of contemporary Manichaeans, who denounced the biblical accounts as grossly materialistic. There is no doubt that Genesis 1–3 contains a number of symbolic features, which predispose interpreters to seek a nonliteral, spiritual meaning behind the text, but how far can that be pushed?

As he matured in his understanding, Augustine came to see that in many cases allegory was being used as a way to escape the potential embarrassments of a literal interpretation, and he reacted against that. In his later years he wrote a commentary on Genesis "according to the letter," in which he sought to correct his earlier enthusiasm for allegory. Whereas he had previously regarded the two trees in the garden of Eden as standing for wisdom (the tree of life) and moderation (the tree of knowledge), he now saw them as real trees in a historical garden. But even so, the tree of life stands for Christ and the tree of the knowledge of good and evil is an awful warning of the consequences of disobeying the commandments of God. Without denying that Adam and Eve had physically eaten the fruit of the latter tree, Augustine nevertheless contrived to interpret the events in largely spiritual terms. He kept his allegorizing under control, but it was allegorizing nonetheless—another indication of just how difficult it was for the fathers to escape it entirely.

But the most interesting aspect of Augustine's interpretation of Genesis is the way in which he saw the creation as the template for the Christian life. Just as human beings are made in the image of God and are restless until they find their rest in him, so the created order also tends toward union with the Creator, which it will achieve on the day of its rest—the Sabbath. He did not think of the six days as a temporal sequence but as a convenient explanation of a single, instantaneous act that had many facets to it. He was willing to grant that our week portrays this within a time frame, but argued that what we perceive as temporal sequence is in reality a hierarchical gradation that is not bound by time or space. The biblical account is both a way of explaining this mystery to finite human minds and a picture of how we ought to grow in our Christian lives.[5]

From the modern point of view, Augustine's attempts to expound the true meaning of Genesis are fascinating because they reveal how complex the problem is. Then as now, interpreters have been forced to wrestle with the juxtaposition of literal and symbolic elements, and knowing how to hold them together is as difficult today as it was back then. The root of the problem is that the rational, analytical mind of Western thought cannot easily grapple with the many

---

5. For a recent treatment of this subject, see Gavin Ortlund, *Retrieving Augustine's Doctrine of Creation: Ancient Wisdom for Current Controversy* (Downers Grove, IL: IVP Academic, 2020).

layers of nuance that are typical of Eastern storytelling. It often appears that our hermeneutical categories are too clumsy to be able to reflect the spirit of the text, where the boundaries between the material and the spiritual are less obvious than we would like them to be. Augustine sensed this but lacked the conceptual apparatus he needed to convey it satisfactorily. He cannot be blamed for this—the subsequent Western tradition has hardly done any better—but more than any of the fathers, he brought the issues to light and presented future generations with a hermeneutical challenge that has still not been definitively resolved.

## THE RULES OF TYCONIUS

Of particular interest to students of patristic exegesis are the rules of Tyconius, which have been transmitted to us by Augustine.[6] That in itself is interesting, since Tyconius was a Donatist and therefore an opponent of Augustine, who wrote a number of treatises against the sect. But Augustine was intelligent enough to realize that although Tyconius was a schismatic and therefore not to be trusted, he was also a clearheaded thinker when it came to literary analysis, and that his hermeneutical principles were deserving of preservation and of imitation even by those who did not follow his particular ecclesiology.

The result is that Augustine devoted a substantial section of his *Christian Instruction* to an analysis of Tyconius, prefacing it with caveats about his orthodoxy and pointing out that Tyconius was not always faithful to his own principles, even as Augustine recommended them for wider use in the church.

Tyconius's first rule is that Scripture speaks of the Lord and his body as a single being. In fact, Christ is the head and the church is his body, but the two are so closely connected that the biblical text

---

6. Augustine of Hippo, *Christian Instruction* 3.30.42–3.37.56.

can pass from one to the other without any indication that it is doing so. The example Augustine gives is Isaiah 61:10, which he reads as "He has placed a garland on me as on a husband and has arrayed me with ornament like a wife." There is only one person talking, yet it is clear that the speaker cannot be both husband and wife at the same time. The answer is that, as head, Christ is the husband, but his body the church is his bride. The interpreter has to know which is which and make the appropriate distinction.

Tyconius's second rule describes what he calls the Lord's two-fold body, meaning by this its heavenly and its earthly dimensions. Augustine objected to this designation because he believed that the material body, being temporal and finite, could not be part of the Lord's eternal body. He would have preferred to make a distinction between what he called the Lord's true body, on the one hand, and his "mixed" or apparent body, on the other. But even that was not really satisfactory, because the Lord's earthly body (the visible church) was a mixed company of true and false believers, and the latter ought not to be included in it. The relevance of this for hermeneutics is that sometimes the Bible speaks about one body when it really means the other. A verse that illustrates this is Song of Songs 1:5 where the bride says, "I am dark and pretty like the tents of Kedar." To Augustine, this makes no sense at the literal level, because it was not possible to be dark and pretty at the same time. But if the text means that the visible church is dark (that is to say, corrupted by the presence of the ungodly within it), it is also pretty by virtue of the elect who are within it. In other words, the visible and the invisible church are conflated into a single reality, but the former is dark and the latter pretty.

Tyconius's third rule concerns the promises and the law. Once again, Augustine tried to improve on this by saying that what he was really talking about was the spirit and the letter of the text, a subject on which Augustine had himself written at some length. Augustine recognized that Tyconius had hit upon an important distinction, but argued that he had failed to appreciate its true significance because he had not been forced to consider the teaching of those who disagreed with him. Augustine, by contrast, had come up against such people in the form of the Pelagians, who believed that it was possible for a person to save himself by his works. Tyconius had said that works are given to us by God in accordance with the measure of our faith, but he had erred by saying that faith itself comes from within us and is not a divine gift. Augustine corrected this mistake by quoting passages such as Ephesians 6:23 and Romans 12:3 and restructured Tyconius's rule accordingly.

The law and the promises are indeed different, but both are gifts of God to be received by faith. As Augustine saw the matter, this adjustment gave Tyconius's rule a force that it did not otherwise have, since it made keeping the law dependent not on a human work of faith but on the divine gift. Since that gift was far stronger than any human assent could ever be, the law of works was correspondingly more compelling and no part of it could be dismissed. In other words, the entire Bible is written for Christians and not just those parts that correspond to our faith, or lack of it.

Tyconius's fourth rule concerns what he called "species" and "genus." By species Tyconius meant a part, and by genus, the whole to which the part belongs. To take the most obvious example, an individual is a species belonging to the universal genus of humanity. This comparison can be extended to other things too, since the Bible sometimes speaks about particular places (like Jerusalem) or nations (like Judea) that it regards as species of the genus of humanity as a whole. The Bible often speaks about species when its message extends to the genus, and the interpreter must be alive to this. The most obvious example is that sometimes we read about Israel, the human nation (species), and at other times about Israel, the people of God (genus). As a species Israel is both blessed and cursed, as the history recorded in the Scriptures makes plain. But the experience of the species is a picture of the promises made to the genus, which includes all the elect children of God. In other words, when the species is promised that it will return to its land and live there in peace for evermore, what the promise really means is that all the ransomed church of God will be saved to sin no more. We must therefore learn to navigate our way from one to the other and interpret the biblical text accordingly.

Tyconius's fifth rule concerns measurements of time, which vary in the Bible and can easily lead to misunderstandings. For example, Christ rose from the dead on the third day according to the Scriptures, but this is true only if we understand the phrase to include the Friday, Saturday, and Sunday. If we think in strictly literal terms, Christ was in the tomb for only about thirty-six hours, or half the time that is suggested by "the third day." It is also the case that the Bible often uses numbers in a symbolic sense, so that to praise God seven times a day (Ps 119:164) means that his praise should be constantly on our lips, not that we should set aside seven particular times for prayer every day.

Tyconius's sixth rule is what he called "recapitulation." This does not mean what it meant to Irenaeus, which was that the New Testament goes back over the history of the Old in order to redeem it, making Jesus the new Adam, Mary the new Eve, and so on. Rather, it refers to a common literary device in the Bible, which we might more readily call "summing up." That is to say that at the end of any given narrative, the text will often go back to the beginning as a way of summing up what the story is all about. This can be disconcerting to those who want the text to proceed from one thing to the next in orderly, chronological sequence, but there is no doubt that the biblical writers did not always follow that pattern, and the sensitive reader must be alert to that.

Tyconius's seventh and final rule is about the devil and his body, which is the negative counterpart of the first rule relating to Christ and his body. Just as Christ and his body the church are often referred to as a single entity, so the devil and fallen humanity are likewise frequently conflated. As a result, what is said of Satan specifically often applies to his followers as well. That is not always the case, but it happens often enough that we must be on our guard not to apply to the devil alone prophecies that include his acolytes and human prisoners.

To the modern reader, Tyconius's rules seem somewhat strange, being a curious mixture of the obvious and the peculiar, and leaving out many things that we would want to put in. If we wanted to evaluate the meaning of a text, we would probably not start from here. But as a study of how one intelligent man in ancient times understood the task of reading and interpreting the Bible, these rules give us a good picture of how he might go about it. As we have already stated, Augustine was not entirely happy with Tyconius, but he took him seriously enough that he was willing to reproduce his principles, albeit with the occasional modification. Tyconius's rules are interesting to us because they bear little relation to Origen's threefold hermeneutic, which was the dominant pattern of biblical interpretation in ancient times. Tyconius showed that another way was possible, and with certain reservations Augustine was prepared to follow him. Of course, it is easy to show that Augustine did not adopt Tyconius's rules consistently—not even Tyconius did that—but it cannot be denied that it was possible to think outside the standard ancient box and that there were great minds prepared to do just that. We might choose a different pattern today, but when faced with the Origenist alternative, many modern people would instinctively lean in Tyconius's direction, just as Augustine did.

## THE CANONIZATION OF PATRISTIC EXEGESIS

By the middle years of the fifth century, it was becoming apparent that the great age of patristic exegesis was drawing to a close. In the West, the great contributions of Jerome and Augustine were impossible to match, and few people saw any need to add to what they had already said. Instead of that, there was a growing desire for anthologies, compendia, and simple question and answer presentations that could resolve some of the difficulties readers of the Bible were likely to encounter. Works of this kind started to proliferate and served as a kind of index to longer and more diffuse writings that few people had either the time or the energy to read. Typical of this period was Eucherius of Lyon (c. 381–455), who wrote what amounts to a dictionary of Bible knowledge arranged by subject matter and taking the reader book by book through both the Old and the New Testaments. He was biased toward allegorical interpretations, but this can be explained by the way he concentrated on phrases like "the eye of the Lord," which obviously could not be understood in a purely literal way. Nothing Eucherius wrote was original to him, but it was presented in a user-friendly way and was particularly useful at a time when the barbarian invasions were wreaking havoc on the civilization of Western Europe.

The continuing popularity of the Psalter can be seen in the abbreviations of Augustine's extensive and somewhat rambling *Enarrations on the Psalms* that were made by Prosper of Aquitaine (c. 390–455) and more comprehensively by Cassiodorus (c. 487–585), who went beyond his master and included material drawn from a wide variety of sources, including Origen and Cyril of Alexandria. He even added comments of his own that supplemented these extracts without contradicting them. Cassiodorus wanted to give the Latin world access to the best commentaries on the Psalms, which to him meant Augustine supplemented by a few others, and that is what he achieved.

The greatest of this new kind of commentator was undoubtedly Bede, who aimed to extend Cassiodorus's approach to the whole of Scripture. Bede thus became the first person to expound a book of the Apocrypha (Tobit) in this systematic way. His commentaries became standard reference works throughout Western Europe and were not finally superseded until the time of the Protestant Reformation.

In the Eastern Christian world the process of anthologization was initiated by Procopius of Gaza (fl. c. 500), whose great commentary on the so-called Octateuch (Genesis–Ruth) set the standard. Procopius deliberately collected extracts from the great commentators of the Greek past and strung them together in a form that would become known as the *catena* ("chain" in Latin). Procopius tells us where he got his material from, which is extremely helpful, since in many cases he cites works that have now been lost. Much of what we know about the history of biblical interpretation in the Greek East has to be reconstructed from the various catenae, and for that reason alone they are invaluable. It is true that on occasion the catenae cite the wrong source, or attribute a text to someone who was copying earlier material, which can sometimes be recovered from the fragments of manuscripts than have been preserved, but this is a relatively minor problem for a history of patristic exegesis. The overall effect of it is to remind us yet again of the enormous debt that the fathers owed to Origen, who often turns out to have been the ultimate source for their observations. It is probable that their dependence on Origen is even greater than we realize, and that would become clear if Origen's lost writings were ever to be found. As it is, that supposition must remain speculative in many cases, but readers have always to be aware that originality was not regarded as a virtue in the ancient world and be prepared to accept that what they find in a fourth or fifth century writer may be much older than they suppose.

Once the catenae began to circulate, the need to copy the original sources was less urgent, and many of them appear to have disappeared progressively over time. Some, like many of Origen's works, were deliberately destroyed, though a few have survived in translations. It is always possible that the sands of Egypt or the library of some ancient monastery may yet turn up one or more of these missing texts and help us fill in some of the gaps in our knowledge, but it is unlikely that our fundamental impression of what patristic exegesis was like will change to any significant degree. We can be fairly confident that we know the essentials already, and that what turns up in the future will merely confirm that and extend the range of examples that we can cite to back up the main framework with which we have long been familiar.

SUMMARY

We can now summarize our findings as follows:

1. In the fourth century there was a reaction against the excesses of allegorical interpretation and a renewed emphasis on the literal sense of the biblical text. This did not lead to an abandonment of the different senses of interpretation but to a desire to reconcile them and understand them as complementary aspects of a single approach to the Bible. In particular, there was a growing tendency to find spiritual application in the material details of the text, which were respected rather than ignored or discounted.

2. The book of Revelation was regarded with suspicion in the Greek-speaking East but much more positively in the Latin-speaking West. This reflected the greater interest that Westerners had in eschatology and the final triumph of the gospel over its enemies.

3. Biblical interpretation in the East came to be codified in a series of extracts that were grouped together as catenae ("chains") which become the standard basis for later interpretation. In the West, the leading figure was Augustine of Hippo, whose hermeneutic was developed on the basis that the Christian life is fellowship with a God of love who has created all things for the benefit of his human creatures. Augustine admired the techniques of literary analysis developed by Tyconius, a schismatic whose approach to the Scriptures was nevertheless close to his own. This synthesis became the basis for medieval biblical interpretation in the western (Latin-speaking) church.

# V

# CASE STUDIES

I t is one thing to talk in general terms about the way the church fathers read the Bible and another to examine more closely what they said about particular passages. A short introduction cannot do justice to the whole of the biblical canon, but those who want a comprehensive overview can now consult the *Ancient Christian Commentary on Scripture*, which covers the material, including the Apocrypha, in twenty-nine volumes.[1] Of course, some passages attracted more attention than others, and they have retained their importance in the life of the church today. Looking at some of them will give us not only a flavor of patristic exegesis but also a sense of how it relates to subsequent, and particularly to modern, approaches to the texts. Opinions will differ as to the extent to which ancient interpretations can be recycled for modern use, but whatever conclusions we may come to about that, knowing how our ancestors

---

1. Thomas C. Oden, ed., *Ancient Christian Commentary on Scripture*, 29 vols. (Downers Grove, IL: InterVarsity Press, 1998–2010).

in the faith understood key biblical texts will provide us with an important resource to illumine our own spiritual understanding.

For the purposes of this study, ten significant texts have been selected for further investigation:

**Old Testament**

| | |
|---|---|
| Genesis 1:26–27 | The image of God |
| 1 Samuel 28:13–14 | Saul and the witch of Endor |
| Psalm 22:1–8 | The cry of dereliction |
| Song of Songs 2:1–4 | The bridegroom and the bride |
| Isaiah 7:14; 9:6 | The messianic oracles |

**New Testament**

| | |
|---|---|
| Matthew 4:1–11 | The temptations of Jesus |
| John 3:3–8 | The new birth |
| Romans 5:12–14 | The nature of sin |
| Hebrews 11:1–3 | The nature of faith |
| Revelation 20:1–6 | The eschatological millennium |

## OLD TESTAMENT

GENESIS 1:26–27

Then God said, "Let us make man in our image, after our likeness. And let them have dominion over the fish of the sea and over the birds of the heavens and over the livestock and over all the earth and over every creeping thing that creeps on the earth."

So God created man in his own image,
    in the image of God he created him;
    male and female he created them.

The narrative of creation was perhaps the most commented on text of Scripture in ancient times, for reasons that we have already explored. At the heart of that narrative is the creation of the human race, which was given a mandate to exercise dominion over the rest of the material world, including both the sea and the air. Nothing is said about spiritual creatures like angels, but we learn from other passages that human beings were considered to be lower than they were, which would seem to exclude any jurisdiction over them.[2] On the other hand, the apostle Paul told the Corinthians that we shall judge the angels, presumably by participating in God's judgment of them (1 Cor 6:3). The fathers did not ignore this functional aspect of creation in God's image, but true to their philosophical inclinations, they were more inclined to focus on what the image tells us about human nature.

According to Clement of Alexandria, to be created in God's image was to be endowed with an eternal soul whose rational faculty has made it possible for us to communicate with God. Jesus Christ, the incarnate Logos or mind of God, was the full and perfect manifestation of the divine image in a human being.[3] A century and a half later, the same theme was reiterated by Marius Victorinus, who insisted that Adam was made "according to the image," the image of the image, so to speak, because only Jesus was the true image of God.[4]

As far as the rest of humanity is concerned, we have all been made in God's image, but most of the fathers regarded this as something distinct from his likeness. They did not have a firm grasp of Hebrew parallelism. Instead of seeing the two terms as virtually synonymous, they preferred to think of the likeness as something extra. Irenaeus believed that Adam and Eve lost the image when they fell because

---

2. Ps 8:5–9, part of which is quoted in Heb 2:7.

3. Clement of Alexandria, *Exhortation to the Greeks* 10.

4. Marius Victorinus, *Against Arius* 1A.20.

they lacked a direct revelation of the Son and therefore could not tell what the true image was like.[5] But most of the fathers thought that God had created Adam and Eve in his image, reserving the acquisition of the likeness to a later stage of growth and perfection that has not yet arrived. As with so much else, this idea seems to be traceable to Origen, who wrote, "The fact that God was silent about the likeness tells us that man received the honor of God's image at his creation, but that the perfection of the divine likeness was reserved for him at the consummation [of all things]. The reason for this was that man had to acquire God's likeness for himself, by earnestly striving to imitate him, so that although he could have obtained perfection through the image, in the end it would be by his works that he would obtain for himself the perfect 'likeness' of God."[6]

Two hundred years later Diadochus of Photice (c. 400–474) claimed that the likeness of God is granted only to those who have subjected their innate freedom to the will of God, because it is only when we no longer belong to ourselves that we can become like him.[7] Meanwhile, Augustine of Hippo put his own interpretation on it by saying that the image of God in humanity is an image of the Trinity, but that this image can never be a perfect likeness because of the fundamental difference between the infinite God and finite human beings.[8] Different again was Gregory of Nyssa, who wrote that we possess God's image by creation but acquire his likeness by exercising our free will. His justification for that was that human beings might thereby become worthy of the reward that comes from God.[9] The Christian life, culminating in the resurrection from the

---

5. Irenaeus, *Against Heresies* 5.16.2.
6. Origen, *First Principles* 3.6.1.
7. Diadochus of Photice, *On Spiritual Perfection* 4.
8. Augustine of Hippo, *The Trinity* 7.6.12.
9. Gregory of Nyssa, *On the Origin of Man*.

dead, was thus interpreted as a process of sanctification that would lead ultimately to the restoration of the divine likeness in those who would be saved.

It is often thought that the fathers regarded women as inferior to men, not least because it was Eve who first responded to the temptation of the serpent, but this is inaccurate. Not all of the fathers commented on human sexual difference, but those who did indicated that the image of God transcended it and applied equally to both male and female, because both were necessary for the completion of humanity and the propagation of the human race. Origen even managed to allegorize this, as we can see from the following: "Our inner man is composed of both spirit and soul. The spirit is male and the soul is female. If they agree with each other, that agreement allows them to increase and multiply so that they produce children—good inclinations and useful ideas—by which they fill the earth and exercise dominion over it."[10] One consequence of this approach was that sexual intercourse was alien to the image of God. John Chrysostom stated that intercourse, and hence the reproduction of the human race, began only after the fall, when the sublime goodness of angelic virginity gave way to the lusts of the flesh.[11]

How much of this can a modern Christian appropriate? It is obvious that the distinction the fathers made between the image and the likeness of God cannot stand up to examination, and so any interpretation based on that must either be abandoned or at least severely modified. But if we confine ourselves to what the fathers had to say about the image, there is much with which we can agree. There is undoubtedly something about human beings that sets us apart from the rest of the material creation and allows us to commune with

---

10. Origen, *Homilies on Genesis* 1.15.

11. John Chrysostom, *Homilies on Genesis* 18.12.

God. The dominion he has given us is real, and we are responsible to him for the way in which we exercise it. It is a privilege granted to all human beings, whether they are believers or not, but as the fathers sensed in their musings about the likeness, there is something different about Christians. We are people who have been enlightened by the truth, and because we possess the Holy Spirit, we can order our lives according to it. We are not perfect, but that the Christian life is a growth in the knowledge and experience of God, none of us would deny. Finally, the image of God is the common possession of both male and female—sexual differentiation makes no difference in terms of our relationship with him. That too, we are more than willing to affirm.

To sum up, although the fathers were mistaken in their analysis of the likeness of God, most of what they had to say about the image is still valid today and needs to be reemphasized in a world where too many have been persuaded that human beings are no more than highly intelligent apes and that all talk of a relationship with God our Creator is essentially mythical.

## 1 SAMUEL 28:13–14

> The king [Saul] said to her [the witch of Endor], "Do not be afraid. What do you see?" And the woman said to Saul, "I see a god coming up out of the earth." He said to her, "What is his appearance?" And she said, "An old man is coming up, and he is wrapped in a robe." And Saul knew that it was Samuel, and he bowed with his face to the ground and paid homage.

This curious story is part of the sorry tale of how Saul, the first king of Israel, fell short of the destiny to which the prophet Samuel had called and anointed him. Among the good things that Saul had done, he had expelled witchcraft from the nation, but after Samuel's death he lost heart in the struggle against his Philistine enemies and went against his own actions. Instead of looking to God, he sought out a medium who could tell him what the future held. He disguised himself so as not to appear to be breaking his own laws, but the medium he approached soon realized who he was. Saul reassured her that she would not get into trouble, and he asked her to conjure up Samuel, the man who had made him king in the first place. Saul got more than he bargained for—not only did Samuel appear, but instead of advising Saul as to how he might overcome the Philistines, he prophesied the king's defeat and death. To modern minds, this story seems alien, though the practice of spiritualism is more common than most of us are prepared to admit. In ancient times, this sort of thing was common and widely accepted, though Jews and Christians recognized its falsity and did what they could to stamp it out.

The fathers knew, of course, that Saul was going against his better judgment and believed that he got what he deserved, but there was another, more immediate dimension to their interpretation of this story. This was the question of whether believers could be brought back after death as a result of witchcraft. Were Christians in the church triumphant in heaven subject to this kind of attack? In other words, was the ghost who came back the real Samuel or a satanic deception? Behind this strange story lay the question of the eternal assurance of the believer, and it was to that issue that the fathers addressed themselves.

The dilemma that confronted the fathers was well expressed by Origen: "If such a great man was indeed under the earth and a medium brought him up, would it not have been the case that a demon had power over the prophet? What can I say? These things are recorded. Is it true or false? To say that it is false encourages unbelief … but to say that it is true presents us with a dilemma."[12]

---

12. Origen, *Homily on 1 Samuel (Kings)* 28.2.2.

Origen was inclined to believe that it was the real Samuel who had been conjured up because to say anything else would be to cast doubt on the truth of God's word. It was hard to believe that Samuel was in hell, but this could be resolved by saying that although Samuel did not deserve to be there, he spent time in the company of sinners for the purpose of saving them. In the end, claimed Origen, the story shows us that there is nowhere that does not need the saving presence of Christ, and the prophets went to hell in order to proclaim that message.[13]

That the souls of the righteous might fall victim to satanic machinations after their deaths was admitted by Justin Martyr, who argued that it explains why Christ taught us to pray that such a fate might not befall us.[14] Tertullian seems to have accepted the possibility that the witch of Endor had been given the power to bring Samuel back from the dead, but he argued that it was a unique case and that, generally speaking, no soul can be called back by a demon.[15] His solution to the problem was somewhat different: "The spirit that created the phantom was no different from the one who made Saul believe in it. The same spirit was in both the witch of Endor and the apostate Saul, so it was easy for him to suggest the lie that he had already made Saul believe [that he was Samuel]. ... Saul saw nothing but the devil, through whom he believed that he would see Samuel."[16]

In the end, Tertullian's objections were overruled and Origen's beliefs were upheld. As Origen himself said, the phantom told the truth and prophesied the future correctly, which a demon could hardly be expected to do.[17] Augustine went further and claimed that

---

13. Origen, *Homily on 1 Samuel (Kings)* 28.7.1.

14. Justin Martyr, *Dialogue with Trypho* 105. See Luke 22:46.

15. Tertullian, *On the Soul* 57.7.

16. Tertullian, *On the Soul* 57.9.

17. Origen, *Homily on 1 Samuel (Kings)* 5.5.8.

it was not impossible for God to send dead people to speak truth to the living. In support of this he cited the story of the transfiguration of Jesus, in which Moses (who was certainly dead) and Elijah appeared alongside him in order to proclaim his divinity. He even mentioned the apocryphal book of Ecclesiasticus, in which Ben Sira, its author, seems to have referred to this incident.[18]

Perhaps the most interesting thing about the patristic interpretation of this passage is that it shows us why the church fathers were so concerned to emphasize that, after his crucifixion, Christ descended into hell. This doctrine is enshrined in the Apostles' Creed, but its biblical basis remains obscure and many people in modern times have questioned its validity. Yet if we reflect that the struggle between good and evil is a holy war that does not cease with our death, because it is spiritual and not physical in nature, we can see why this strange story captured the imagination of the fathers as much as it did. In fact, the dilemma that Origen flagged has never been satisfactorily resolved. On the one hand, there is the question of the truth of Scripture: If the text says that it was Samuel who appeared to Saul, do we not have to take it at face value? On the other hand, how can we believe that God's people are subject to evil powers after their death? What becomes of the assurance of salvation, not to mention the sovereignty of God, if we accept a doctrine like that?

Perhaps the answer lies in the words of the writer to the Hebrews, who lists the great saints of the Old Testament, including Samuel, only to end by saying that they "did not receive what was promised, since God had provided something better for us, that apart from us they should not be made perfect" (Heb 11:39–40). The church fathers believed that Samuel, along with the other saints of ancient Israel, were

---

18. Augustine of Hippo, *The Care to Be Taken for the Dead* 15.18. See Matt 17:3; Sir 46:16–20.

in a holding pattern until the coming of Christ, when at last, like us, they were able to enter into the joy of their Lord and be set free from the kind of attack that befell Samuel at the hands of the witch of Endor.

PSALM 22:1–8

My God, my God, why have you forsaken me?
    Why are you so far from saving me, from the words of
        my groaning?
O my God, I cry by day, but you do not answer,
    and by night, but I find no rest.

Yet you are holy,
    enthroned on the praises of Israel.
In you our fathers trusted;
    they trusted, and you delivered them.
To you they cried and were rescued;
    in you they trusted and were not put to shame.

But I am a worm and not a man,
    scorned by mankind and despised by the people.
All who see me mock me;
    they make mouths at me; they wag their heads;
"He trusts in the LORD; let him deliver him;
    let him rescue him, for he delights in him!"

The psalmist's cry of dereliction might have gone more or less unnoticed had it not been quoted by Jesus on the cross (Matt 27:46; Mark 15:34). Needless to say, it was that quotation that governed the fathers' interpretation of the verse in its original context and provided them with clear evidence that, not only this psalm, but that the Psalms as a whole were essentially christological in nature. They may have originated in the words of King David and the great singers of Israel, but those men were prophets who spoke of Christ long before anyone knew that he was coming. The first verse of Psalm 22 in particular was the way into a much broader hermeneutic that over time embraced not only the psychology of Jesus but also the spiritual experience of believers.

The relationship between David and Jesus was clearly outlined by Leo the Great of Rome: "King David preceded the day of the Lord's crucifixion by more than 1,100 years. He had suffered none of the tortures that he mentions as having been inflicted on himself. Because the Lord [Jesus] was going to take his suffering flesh from David's stock, spoke through his mouth, the story of the crucifixion has rightly been foreshadowed in the person of David. David bore in himself the bodily origin of the Savior. David genuinely suffered in Christ because Christ was genuinely crucified in the flesh of David."[19]

The inapplicability of the psalm to any ancient Israelite king or prophet was also mentioned by Eusebius of Caesarea, the great historian of the early church, who concluded, as all his fellow Christians did, that its words described nobody other than the suffering Savior himself.[20] But although this point was generally recognized, the fathers were also inclined to see the words of Jesus in this psalm as spoken in his capacity as the representative of sinful humanity in general. One anonymous writer, whose work has come down to us under the name of Athanasius, wrote, "[Jesus] asks the Father to turn his face toward us, to remove sin and its curse from us, and to teach us humility, just as he himself was humbled for our sake."[21] Augustine said exactly the same thing.[22] Gregory of

---

19. Leo the Great, *Sermon* 67.1.

20. Eusebius of Caesarea, *Demonstration of the Gospel* 10.8.492.

21. Pseudo-Athanasius, *Exposition of the Psalms* 22.

22. Augustine of Hippo, *Expositions on the Psalms* 22.

Nazianzus developed it further: "[Jesus] was in his own person representing us. We were the ones who were forsaken and despised, but now, by the sufferings of him who could not suffer, we have been taken up and saved. He makes our folly and our transgressions his own."[23] In these remarks of the fathers we can see how two originally distinct themes have come together. On the one hand there is the fulfillment of prophecy with respect to the nation of Israel and the covenant made with David, while on the other hand there is the more universal appeal of the gospel. Christ died for the sins of the whole world by becoming a substitute for us. In their exposition of Psalm 22 the fathers thus expressed the doctrine of substitutionary atonement, which in later times would become the cornerstone of the doctrine of redemption.

The fathers well understood that, as the Son of God, Jesus could not have suffered and died in his divine nature, and so Psalm 22 was a clear expression of his incarnation as a human being. Even Cyril of Alexandria, who believed that the Son had united human flesh to himself in a single nature, and whose teaching would lead (after his death) to division in the Eastern church between those who confessed two natures in the incarnate Christ and those who did not, saw this very clearly. As he put it, "[Christ] made his own the sufferings of his flesh in his crucified body, impassibly, for by the grace of God and for the sake of all people he tasted death, surrendering his own body to it, even though by nature he was life and the resurrection."[24]

Of course, for those who accepted the two-nature Christology of the Council of Chalcedon, there was no difficulty in ascribing the Father's "abandonment" of the Son to the latter's human nature. A century or so before Chalcedon, Eusebius had already said that

---

23. Gregory of Nazianzus, *Orations* 30.5.

24. Cyril of Alexandria, *Letters* 17.11.

the Father had forsaken his Son in order that the Son could ransom the human race by buying them back from the slavery of sin by the shedding of his blood.[25] Later on, and in the wake of Chalcedon, Theodoret of Cyrrhus summed it all up by saying, "Just as the one who was a fount of righteousness assumed our sin, … accepted our curse and willingly endured the shame of the cross, so too he uttered these words on our behalf."[26] Once again, this is penal substitutionary atonement in all but name. In the eyes of the world, Christ had become like a worm, despised by those who could not understand how a crucified man could be the Lord and Savior of the world, yet it was in and through this wonderful humility that the new humanity came into being.[27]

It is thanks to the witness of the Gospels that Psalm 22 has been consistently interpreted in terms of Christ's atoning sacrifice, and the fathers cannot be faulted for having indulged in allegory here. This is not to say that they were free of all speculation, as we can see from Eusebius, who thought that one of the reasons the Father forsook Christ on the cross was so that the latter's love for the people he had come to save might shine out more clearly.[28] It is an odd idea and there is no evidence in the texts for drawing such a conclusion, but it is not an allegorical fantasy. Christ did indeed love those for whom he died, even if it did not require the Father's abandonment of him to demonstrate that. Modern Christians can therefore appropriate the patristic interpretation of Psalm 22 with few reservations and recognize that the vital truths of our salvation have withstood the test of time.

---

25. Eusebius of Caesarea, *Demonstration of the Gospel* 10.8.495.

26. Theodoret of Cyrrhus, *Commentary on the Psalms* 22.3.

27. Augustine of Hippo, *Sermons* 380.2.

28. Eusebius of Caesarea, *Demonstration of the Gospel* 10.8.496.

SONG OF SONGS 2:1–4

> I am a rose of Sharon,
>   a lily of the valleys.
>
> As a lily among brambles,
>   so is my love among the young women.
>
> As an apple tree among the trees of the forest,
>   so is my beloved among the young men.
> With great delight I sat in his shadow,
>   and his fruit was sweet to my taste.
> He brought me to the banqueting house,
>   and his banner over me was love.

No book of the Bible, with the exception of Revelation, has been subjected to a wider variety of interpretations than the Song of Songs. But whereas Revelation is otherworldly to begin with and almost invites allegorical readings, the Song of Songs is—at least on the surface—a poem, or series of poems, celebrating earthly love. What was it doing in the Bible, which is a collection of texts that constitute a revelation from God? God is never mentioned in the Song, but none of the church fathers could accept that it was not part of his eternal word to them. Nor could most of them believe that it should be read in the literal sense. To their minds, the Song was a supreme allegory of the love between Christ and his bride, who might be the church or the individual believer. There is ground for this interpretation in the New Testament, where the church is portrayed as a bride awaiting the return of her husband, the risen, ascended, and glorified Christ (Rev 21:2).

There is therefore some scriptural logic to the fathers' allegorization of the text, however extravagant it may seem at times. It can also be said that although alternative readings have been proposed, especially in modern times, it is the allegorical one that has lasted the longest and made the deepest impression on later generations of Christians. Even today, Song 2:4 has been turned into a popular chorus ("He brought me into his banqueting house and his banner over me is love"), which those who sing it automatically apply to their new relationship to Christ as their Lord and Savior. They do not have to be told to do this, and most people probably have no idea that the verse they are singing comes from the Song of Songs, but the fact that they interpret it christologically, without any prompting, shows that the ancient allegory is far from dead.

The Septuagint translation of the first verse says "flower of the field" instead of "rose of Sharon," though the meaning is much the same. Ambrose of Milan regarded the field as the plain simplicity of a pure mind, which he said was a place that Christ liked to dwell because he is a model of simplicity and lowliness.[29] The application here is clearly to the heart and mind of individual believers, especially those who have experienced the brambles of trouble and sorrow in their lives. Ambrose even went so far as to say that when the flower is cut off, it does not lose its odor, comparing this to the suffering and death of Christ, who was cut off by his death but at the same time made more beautiful by the color of his outpoured blood, which made him able to impart the gift of eternal life to those who believe in him.[30]

Nilus of Ancyra understood the valleys to mean the lower parts of the earth's surface and contrasted them with the field in which the flower originally grew. To his mind, that field was Israel, which had been prepared by the teachings of the Law and the Prophets for spiritual cultivation, whereas the valleys were the gentiles, previously

---

29. Ambrose of Milan, *On Virginity* 9.51.
30. Ambrose of Milan, *The Holy Spirit* 2.38–39.

barren and unfruitful, but now increasingly productive as the sowers
of God's word went out to plant the seed in them.[31] The same theme
was developed further by Theodoret of Cyrrhus, who portrayed
Christ as bringing salvation to the living (the field) and also resurrection to the dead (the valleys), though he did not identify the living
and the dead with Israel and the gentiles in the way that Nilus did.[32]

The seamless transition from the struggles of the individual to
those of the church can be seen in the way that Augustine interpreted
the brambles. Following his master, Ambrose, who described the lily
as pure virtue surrounded by the spiritual wickedness of the thorns,
he did not hesitate to label the latter as heretics, who in the guise of
young women ("daughters" in the LXX) put on a show of worshiping
Christ while in reality subverting his teaching at every opportunity.[33] His advice to his congregation was clear: "Be a lily; receive the
mercy of God. Hold fast to the root of a good flower, and do not be
ungrateful for the soft rain that comes from heaven. It is the thorns
who will be ungrateful. They too grow in the rain, but they do so
in order to be thrown on the fire, not stored in the barn."[34] As time
went on, it became conventional to interpret the lily as the church
and the apple tree as a blessing that provided shade for the weary
and for the healing of the sick.[35]

It is in the fourth verse that we reach the climax of the love relationship between Christ and his bride. The fathers were quick to
point out that love is not restricted to our relationship with God
but manifests itself in many ways, especially within the family. This

---

31. Nilus of Ancyra, *Commentary on the Song of Songs* 39–40.

32. Theodoret of Cyrrhus, *Commentary on the Song of Songs* 2.

33. Ambrose of Milan, *Concerning Virgins* 1.8.43; Augustine of Hippo, *Sermons* 37.27.

34. Augustine of Hippo, *Enarrations on the Psalms* 48.8.

35. Gregory the Great, *Forty Gospel Homilies* 38; Ambrose of Milan, *Six Days of Creation* 3.17.71.

is perfectly right and proper, but the Christian must always put the love of God above the natural affection that we have for our parents, siblings, and neighbors.[36] The fathers' knowledge of secular society left them with no illusions about what went on in the banqueting house, but they turned this to their advantage, as we can see quite clearly in the praise showered on the bride by Nilus of Ancyra: "The bride alone had believed in the grape cluster hanging on the cross, when it was counted for nothing because it had not yet exhibited the properties of wine. She alone had believed in this grape cluster, although its true identity would not become clear until a later time. She had worked out an idea so exalted, long before the onset of the wine season, that allowed her to discern the future wine even in the flowering vine. ... This is why she asks to be given the exceptional privilege of entry into the house of wine."[37]

What should we make of this? The essence of allegory is that it superimposes theological truths onto texts that appear to have little or nothing to do with them. In this respect, allegory is similar to astrology, which purports to discern human destiny in the movement of the stars, when in reality the two are unconnected. But whereas the astrologer is abusing scientific facts in order to promote a form of pastoral counseling, the interpreter of the Song is dealing with poetry that is already removed from the literal realities that it describes. Whatever we make of the beloved, she was not a lily of the field, nor was she an apple tree. At the very least, these are metaphors for something else, and if we find the application to Christ and the church somewhat excessive at times, it is not in principle to be excluded. Let us admit that the fathers were sometimes carried away by their rhetoric, and that as preachers they often produced

---

36. Augustine of Hippo, *Sermons* 50 (100).2; 344.2; Bede, *On the Tabernacle* 1.6.
37. Nilus of Ancyra, *Commentary on the Song of Songs* 45.

applications that went beyond what the text can reasonably justify. But that human love at its best is still only a pale reflection of God's love surely cannot be denied, and it is that which interested the fathers above all else. It is also that which should concern us, and in that respect the patristic interpretation of the Song of Songs still has something to teach us today.

ISAIAH 7:14; 9:6

> The Lord himself will give you a sign. Behold, the virgin shall conceive and bear a son, and shall call his name Immanuel.

> For to us a child is born,
>     to us a son is given;
> and the government shall be upon his shoulder,
>     and his name shall be called
> Wonderful Counselor, Mighty God,
>     Everlasting Father, Prince of Peace.

That Isaiah is the greatest of the prophets of the Old Testament is universally acknowledged, though many modern commentators see his book as a collection of oracles given by different people over the course of several centuries rather than as the work of the prophet who lived in the eighth century BC. The church fathers knew nothing of that, of course—to them Isaiah was the man who preached in the time of King Hezekiah and his immediate predecessors. They knew that much of what he said referred to what was (to him) a distant future, but that belief did not lead them to suspect later hands at work on the text. On the contrary, it increased their respect for him as a prophet, and they quoted him frequently, and sometimes at considerable length, in defense of their belief that the messianic oracles had been fulfilled in the life, death, and resurrection of Jesus

Christ. From their point of view, the book of Isaiah was the clearest statement of the gospel to be found in the Old Testament, and they used it (in the Greek LXX version, of course) for much of their own preaching and teaching ministry. In this, they were following the example of the New Testament writers, while adding to their statements and elaborating on their themes as they thought appropriate.

It is well known that the church fathers knew little or no Hebrew, and in the case of Isaiah 7:14 this matters more than it usually does elsewhere. The Greek text translates the Hebrew word *ʾalmah* as *parthenos* (virgin), whereas the more common Hebrew word for that was *bethulah*. There was therefore an argument between Jews and Christians about the interpretation of this verse, and Christians were not slow to defend their interpretation. Jerome, for example, recognized the difficulty but claimed that *ʾalmah* was not simply a "young woman" as the Jews insisted. To his mind, the Hebrew word for that was *naʿarah*, whereas *ʾalmah* was a "hidden virgin." He understood this to mean a virgin plus something extra, because not every virgin lives in seclusion as an *ʾalmah* supposedly did.[38]

More convincing is the explanation attributed to Theophylact of Ochrid (c. 1050–1108), who lived some centuries later but whose opinion probably goes back to a much earlier time, since echoes of it can be found in John Chrysostom (late fourth century).[39] Theophylact wrote, "'Young woman' and 'virgin' mean the same thing in Scripture, because a young woman is one who is still a virgin. If it was not a virgin who gave birth, how would it have been an extraordinary sign?"[40] Theophylact believed that the Jews had altered the text because of their antipathy toward Christians, but

---

38. Jerome, *Against Jovinianus* 1.32.

39. John Chrysostom, *Homilies on the Gospel of Matthew* 5.3.

40. Theophylact of Ochrid, *Explanation of Matthew* 23.

although he was wrong about that, it is true that the Hebrew text used in the synagogues in his day had been edited well after the rise of Christianity, so some such modification could not be automatically ruled out.

For the most part, the fathers regarded the virgin birth—or, more properly, virginal conception—of Christ as proof of God's activity in their midst. As Justin Martyr explained, "By the prophetic Spirit, God announced the coming of unimaginable things, things that are impossible in human terms, so that when it happened people would believe and accept it by faith because it had been promised."[41] Conscious of the many myths in which pagan gods consorted with human women, Justin was careful to add that the virginal conception of Christ took place without intercourse of any kind. As he put it, "God's power came on the virgin, overshadowed her and caused her to conceive while she remained a virgin."[42] The spiritual significance of this was not lost on Tertullian, who saw in it the beginning of a new humanity: "God was born as man, taking the flesh of the old human race, but without the aid of the old human seed. God took the flesh in order to reform the old human race with a new seed. In other words, he spiritually cleansed the old human race by removing its old stains."[43]

As for the sort of government the child would exercise, Justin Martyr was in no doubt. The government was upon his shoulders, Justin said, because Christ carried his cross on his shoulders and that was the essence of his rule.[44] Later on, Ambrose of Milan said something similar but with his own particular twist: "The passion

---

41. Justin Martyr, *First Apology* 33.
42. Justin Martyr, *First Apology* 33.
43. Tertullian, *The Flesh of Christ* 17.
44. Justin Martyr, *First Apology* 35.

of Christ's body is either the power of his divinity or the cross that towers over his body. He bowed his shoulder, applying himself to the plow—patient in enduring insults and so subject to affliction that it was for our wickedness that he was wounded, and for our sins that he was weakened."[45] Bede, writing at the end of the patristic era, summed up the government of Christ by saying that it was for the reconciliation of the world to God that the Son became incarnate. It was for that that he suffered and was raised from the dead, making peace between us and God by his act of reconciliation.[46]

Once again, we find Jerome having recourse to the Hebrew original in order to point out the inadequacies of the Septuagint translation. According to him, the Greek translators were so terrified of calling a child "God" that, instead of the six names by which he was to be glorified, they put "angel of great counsel, and I will bring peace and his salvation upon the princes."[47] As a result of this mistranslation, many of the fathers, both Greek and Latin, found themselves commenting on the "angel of great counsel," even though that phrase does not appear in the original. Typical of this approach was Novatian, a third-century Latin writer, who said that the title of angel suited Christ because not only was he the Son of God but he was also a messenger, being the herald of the Father's dispensation of salvation.[48]

Novatian was right in what he said, of course, but he based it on a faulty reading of the text. This is a reminder to us of something that was more common in ancient times than we like to admit. Few people could be absolutely certain that they had correct readings of

---

45. Ambrose of Milan, *The Patriarchs* 6.31.

46. Bede, *Homilies on the Gospels* 2.9.

47. Jerome, *Commentary on Isaiah* 3.9.17.

48. Novatian, *The Trinity* 18.9–10.

the Scriptures. The general message was clear enough and quite consistent throughout, but as commentators and preachers probed into particular words and phrases, they were not infrequently met with difficulties and obscurities that were due more to mistranslation or to inaccurate copying than to anything else. What they relied on in such situations was the general sense of Christian teaching, applying it to passages that (strictly speaking) could not support it.

This is why we must always be cautious when reading the fathers and relying on their interpretations. They may be right in theological and doctrinal terms but mistaken in purely exegetical ones. They cannot be blamed for this, but neither should their opinions be given more weight than they deserve. The scholarship of later times has helped us see the fathers more clearly than we might otherwise have done, and if it too sometimes oversteps the mark, it should be seen as a resource for greater understanding of the ancient tradition, not as an enemy to it or as a straightforward replacement for it.

## NEW TESTAMENT

### MATTHEW 4:1–11

Jesus was led up by the Spirit into the wilderness to be tempted by the devil. And after fasting forty days and forty nights, he was hungry. And the tempter came and said to him, "If you are the Son of God, command these stones to become loaves of bread." But he answered, "It is written,

"'Man shall not live by bread alone,

but by every word that comes from the mouth of God.' "
[Deut 8:3]

Then the devil took him to the holy city and set him on the pinnacle of the temple and said to him, "If you are the Son of God, throw yourself down, for it is written,

"'He will command his angels concerning you,' [Ps 91:11]
    and
"'On their hands they will bear you up,
    lest you strike your foot against a stone.' " [Ps 91:12]

Jesus said to him, "Again it is written, 'You shall not put the Lord your God to the test.' " [Deut 6:16] Again, the devil took him to a very high mountain and showed him all the kingdoms of the world and their glory. And he said to him, "All these I will give you, if you will fall down and worship me." Then Jesus said to him, "Be gone, Satan! For it is written,

"'You shall worship the Lord your God
    and him only shall you serve.' " [Deut 6:13]

Then the devil left him, and behold, angels came and were ministering to him.

The temptations of Jesus have long been something of a puzzle to Christians. If he was the Son of God, how could the devil have been allowed to tempt him like this? Matthew put the incident at the beginning of Jesus' public ministry and revealed to his readers that it was by the Holy Spirit that he went into the desert in the first place. Trials of that kind were not uncommon, and the Bible tells us that many great men spent time in the wilderness, preparing (or being prepared) for their ministry—Moses, Elijah, John the Baptist, and the apostle Paul among them. But Jesus, the Son of God, was in a class of his own. He did not need to be spiritually refined for his future service, but humbled himself to do battle with Satan. The struggle between good and evil is not an equal one—Satan could never hope to defeat God—but it is a reality that we all have to face, and the church fathers saw in this incident one of the key ingredients of their own spiritual lives.

John Chrysostom pointed out that Jesus was led by the Spirit and commented, "All this was for our instruction. The Lord does whatever is necessary for our salvation. ... We must not be troubled if we have to endure great temptations, even after our baptism. We should not regard this as something unexpected but courageously endure whatever comes our way, as if it were part of the natural order of things."[49]

Hilary of Poitiers made great play of the forty days of fasting that preceded the temptations and did not hesitate to draw analogies with the experiences of other human beings. As he put it, "The Lord was tempted immediately after his baptism. The temptation indicates how nefarious the devil's attacks against those who have been sanctified are, for he is eager to claim victory over the saints. Jesus did not hunger for human food, but for human salvation, and that was only after forty days. Moses and Elijah were not hungry when they fasted, so when the Lord hungered, it was not because his abstinence had got the better of him. His strength was not diminished by his forty days of fasting."[50] The message was clear. Physical self-discipline, if conducted in the right spirit, would not make it inevitable that we should be defeated by spiritual temptation. The devil might try to exploit the weakness of our flesh, but with the help of God we can overcome him, as Jesus did.

Origen also focused attention on the forty days, which he subdivided into four groups of ten, corresponding to the four elements of

---

49. John Chrysostom, *Homilies on the Gospel of Matthew* 13.1.

50. Hilary of Poitiers, *On Matthew* 3.2.

the physical creation (earth, air, water, and fire).[51] The anonymous author of an incomplete commentary on Matthew, traditionally ascribed to John Chrysostom, claimed that the forty-day period was set for two reasons. The first was so that Jesus could give us an example of fasting as a means of warding off temptations, and the second was to set a limit to it so that we should not overdo our self-deprivation.[52] Peter Chrysologus (380–450) tied all this together and linked it to the Lenten fast: "So you see that the fact that we fast during Lent is not a human invention. We have it on divine and mystical authority. ... The forty days of Lent represent the four-sided teaching of four decades of faith, because perfection is always four-sided. The numbers forty and ten contain mysteries in heaven and earth, because a square is not free to open, and so they are used to expound the meaning of the Lord's fasting."[53]

When speaking about Satan's encounter with Christ, the fathers tended to assert that the devil was unaware of whom he was dealing with. Hilary of Poitiers spoke of Satan's "suspicious fear" but claimed that he had no knowledge of the one whom he suspected.[54] Chromatius (c. 400) filled this out further: "Satan was frightened, but did not fully believe that the Son of God, of whom he had heard and whom he was now looking at in the flesh, would take away the sins of the world. ... He remembered that Moses and Elijah had also fasted for forty days, and so wanted some sign that would prove that Jesus was the Son of God [and therefore greater than them]."[55] John Chrysostom was more subtle than this. He suggested that Satan

51. Origen, *Fragment* 61. See Manlio Simonetti, ed., *Matthew 1–13*, vol. 1a of *Ancient Christian Commentary on Scripture: New Testament* (Downers Grove, IL: InterVarsity Press, 2001), 67.

52. *Incomplete Work on Matthew* 5.

53. Peter Chrysologus, *Sermons* 11.4.

54. Hilary of Poitiers, *On Matthew* 3.1.

55. Chromatius, *Tractate on Matthew* 14.2.

thought he could succeed by ignoring the fact that Jesus was hungry and flattering him by mentioning only his supposed dignity as the Son of God. But Jesus countered this strategy by moving the discussion from the lusts of the flesh to the power of the Spirit, pointing out that man does not live by bread alone.[56] Did Satan not realize that? Apparently not!

That the food of the Christian was a heavenly gift far surpassing anything that we might desire to eat on earth was a commonplace running through the writings of the fathers from Origen onward. Origen himself contrasted earthly bread with the heavenly manna that fed the children of Israel in the wilderness, and applied it to the first temptation of Jesus.[57] Maximus of Turin (d. c. 408–423) spelled it out clearly: "Whoever feeds on the word of Christ does not need earthly food, nor can someone who eats the bread of Christ desire the food of the world. The Lord has his own bread; indeed, the bread is the Savior himself, who came down from heaven."[58] Jerome too, though he refrains from recommending fasting, nevertheless used this incident to make the point that anyone who does not feed on God's word will not live, as the quotation from Deuteronomy made plain.[59]

When commenting on the second temptation, the fathers were quick to notice that Satan approached Jesus with the same weapon that Jesus had already used to fend him off—the testimony of Scripture. But as Jerome pointed out, Satan was a poor interpreter of the sacred text, applying to the Son of God words that were meant to refer to a holy man and neglecting to add that the person so empowered would trample the serpent underfoot. Jerome knew that

---

56. John Chrysostom, *Homilies on the Gospel of Matthew* 13.3.

57. Origen, *Fragmenta in Matthaeum*, 63. See Simonetti, *Matthew 1–13*, 59.

58. Maximus of Turin, *Sermons* 51.2. See John 6:41.

59. Jerome, *Commentary on Matthew* 1.4.4.

Satan would not want to predict his own downfall and so resorted to selective quotation of a text that, if properly understood, prophesied just that.[60] Jesus' response was to quote Deuteronomy in its true sense, and John Chrysostom drew the lesson for his hearers. However provoked a Christian might be by the enemies of God, no one should ever try to overcome the devil by a show of spiritual power. The weapons of our warfare are patience and longsuffering, against which Satan can do nothing.[61]

It was left to Gregory the Great, however, to develop this principle fully. As Gregory said, "When the Lord was tempted by the devil, he answered him with the commands of the sacred Scriptures. By the Word that he was, he could easily have cast his tempter into outer darkness, but he did not do that. Instead, he did no more than quote the teaching of Scripture. This was to set an example for us, so that when we are attacked we should teach rather than seek revenge. ... The Lord endured the devil's opposition and he answered him with nothing but words of gentleness."[62] The fathers were very alert to the power of rhetoric, and the fact that there were three graded temptations did not escape their notice. The first was aimed at the body and the desire for food, the second at the soul and the desire for fame, and the third at the spirit, with its lust for power. Once again, it was Gregory the Great who expressed this in the greatest detail, but in doing so he was merely recapitulating what many others had said before him.

When we look at the way the fathers interpreted the temptations of Jesus, what strikes us most is the fact that they almost always related them to the disciplines and temptations of the Christian life.

---

60. Jerome, *Commentary on Matthew* 1.4.6.

61. John Chrysostom, *Homilies on the Gospel of Matthew* 13.4.

62. Gregory the Great, *Forty Gospel Homilies* 16.3.

The logic behind that was that Jesus, as God, could not be tempted at all, so that it was only as a man that he had to face the wiles of the devil. That in turn made his temptations a model for our spiritual lives, since we too are tempted as he was and can learn from his response how to deal with that. It does not seem to have occurred to any of the fathers that the temptations of Jesus were unique to him and that their very nature bears witness to his divinity. We can only be tempted to do what is possible, and no human being can turn stones into bread! It is hard to know why the fathers did not mention this, but the answer may be that it was because they portrayed the devil as being ignorant of Jesus' true identity. Yet if Satan did not know who he was, why would he have tempted him to do something that only God can do? There is something of a logical disconnect here, which may be explained by the fathers' concentration on the human Jesus setting an example for us, rather than on the divine Son of God being revealed even by the machinations of his archenemy.

JOHN 3:3–8

> Jesus answered Nicodemus, "Truly, truly, I say to you, unless one is born again he cannot see the kingdom of God. Nicodemus said to him, "How can a man be born when he is old? Can he enter a second time into his mother's womb and be born?" Jesus answered, "Truly, truly, I say to you, unless one is born of water and the Spirit, he cannot enter the kingdom of God. That which is born of the flesh is flesh, and that which is born of the Spirit is spirit. Do not marvel that I said to you, 'You must be born again.' The wind blows where it wishes, and you hear its sound, but you do not know where it comes from or where it goes. So it is with everyone who is born of the Spirit."

To enter the Christian church was to begin a new life. No longer would there be Jews and gentiles, slaves and free people. All would be one in Christ. Differences would remain, to be sure, but they would no longer be barriers. Christians would constitute a single body, of which Christ was the head. What would make this possible was the belief that everyone who professed the faith of Christ in sincerity and truth would be born again, not in the physical sense, but in the spiritual one. What did this mean and how could it be perceived? Jewish males bore the sign of circumcision that marked them off as members of the chosen people, but this was not true of Christians. On the other hand, to become a Christian was to be baptized in water, on profession of faith. Was this the same thing as being born again? What was the relationship between the sacrament, as Tertullian called it, and the reality that it signified? These questions have resurfaced throughout church history and are still vigorously debated today. What do the fathers of the church have to contribute to that debate?

When comparing natural human birth to its spiritual equivalent, Justin Martyr was blunt: "We were born without our knowledge or choice ... and brought up with bad habits. But we may become the children of choice and knowledge, and obtain forgiveness of our sins in the water [of baptism]. ... This washing is called illumination because those who receive it are illuminated in their understanding."[63] In fairness to Justin, he lived at a time when nobody would be baptized unless they were already converted, and when the act of baptism signified a real change of outward life as well as inward renewal. In such circumstances it was easy to believe that the two things went together—nominal Christians were few and far between. Later on, a more sophisticated approach began to appear. Gregory of Nazianzus

---

63. Justin Martyr, *First Apology* 61.

said that the new birth comes from the Holy Spirit and produces the new creation, which in turn gives us a deeper knowledge of God. There is no suggestion that physical immersion in water effects spiritual regeneration, without further ado. Theodore of Mopsuestia put it like this: "The work of generation is necessarily consonant with the nature of the generator. When flesh begets flesh, the generation in necessarily corporeal. When the Spirit generates, the generation must be incorporeal and spiritual. The water that is united with the Spirit does not operate with him but is mentioned as a symbol for a visible use. That is why Jesus did not talk about what was born of water, but only about what is born of the Spirit, to whom he clearly attributed the work of generation."[64]

Nevertheless, a certain ambiguity remained, as can be seen from comments on the matter made by John Chrysostom. On the one hand, Chrysostom was insistent on the need for water baptism, because by it the promises of our covenant with God are realized—burial and death, resurrection and new life all happen simultaneously.[65] On the other hand, he stressed that the new creation out of water was a mystery that required the direct operation of the Holy Spirit. Water might be the starting point, but it was nothing in and of itself and would have no effect if God did not use it to bring about the new person in Christ.[66]

Augustine was particularly exercised by the question put to him about the children of believers. If they were new creations in Christ, why did they not produce children who were born again from the moment of conception? The answer, of course, was that parents can only pass on to their children what they are in Adam—people of flesh who have fallen into sin by disobedience to the commandment

---

64. Theodore of Mopsuestia, *Commentary on John* 2.3.6.

65. John Chrysostom, *Homilies on the Gospel of John* 25.2.

66. John Chrysostom, *Homilies on the Gospel of John* 25.1.

of God. Spiritual rebirth can never be a mechanical thing but must be the gift of the Holy Spirit, without which it cannot take place.[67]

The comparison Jesus makes between the Spirit and the wind was perhaps the clearest indication of the essential difference between water and Spirit in baptism. Anyone can perform the outward act of immersion, but the work of the Spirit is beyond human control or even understanding. Hilary of Poitiers remarked that the Spirit has no limitations. The Spirit says what he wants, when he wants, and where he wants. We recognize his presence when he is with us, but we cannot explain why he comes and goes in the way he does.[68] Theodore of Mopsuestia sums it up magnificently: "The Holy Spirit is all-powerful. He does exactly what he wants, and nothing can resist his working. You can hear his voice and perceive that he is coming, but you cannot pin him down or understand how he operates. He is ungraspable by nature, and so is everywhere he chooses to be. Likewise, his action is beyond our understanding, because he does everything according to his own will."[69]

The experience of centuries of nominal Christianity has made us more sensitive than the fathers were to the potential superficiality of water baptism. In the ancient church, nobody questioned the baptism of infants apart from Tertullian, and then it was because he believed that it was unfair to cleanse a baby from sin when it did not know what was happening to it. Tertullian was afraid that the child would grow up in ignorance of her perfect state and sin again, thereby losing her salvation! That is certainly not the way that modern Baptists think. The fathers were generally prepared to baptize anyone who came to the church requesting it, including those who were presented by their parents, but they were well aware that matters did not end there. Just as

---

67. Augustine of Hippo, *Tractates on the Gospel of John* 11.6.1; *Sermons* 174.9, 294.16.

68. Hilary of Poitiers, *On the Trinity* 12.56.

69. Theodore of Mopsuestia, *Commentary on John* 2.3.7–8.

a child had to grow in the life that was given to her, so the believer had to do the same.[70] If that did not happen, there was no new birth at all.

The fathers did not have to preach the gospel to a world in which many were outwardly baptized but inwardly far from God. To them, the rite was a sacred transition from the world to the church, and through the church to the kingdom of heaven. There are modern believers who still subscribe to that analogy, but the reality of everyday life forces us to admit that the ideal is all too often negated in practice. In appropriating patristic teachings on this subject, we must always bear in mind the very different circumstances in which we live. We cannot know what Chrysostom or Augustine would have said if they had been confronted with our situation, but their emphasis on the Spirit gives a clue to their approach. Only that which is born of the Spirit is spirit—nothing else, however symbolic and supportive it may be, can take his place.

ROMANS 5:12–14

> Therefore, just as sin came into the world through one man, and death through sin, and so death spread to all men because all sinned—for sin indeed was in the world before the law was given, but sin is not counted where there is no law. Yet death reigned from Adam to Moses, even over those whose sinning was not like the transgression of Adam, who as a type of the one who was to come.

It may come as a surprise to modern readers, but the question of sin and the origin of evil was a major issue in ancient times. The Greco-Roman world tended to think that matter was evil and that only nonmaterial things were "good." This is why the Greeks developed

---

70. Augustine of Hippo, *Sermons* 71.19.

philosophy in the way they did—it was an attempt to rise above the earth and enter the realm of ideas, where alone perfection could be found. The biblical worldview was completely different. According to Genesis, God created everything good, according to its nature. Evil was a spiritual rebellion against him, led by the angel Satan, who tempted the first human beings to follow him in rejecting the law of God. As a result of that, the human race descended from Adam and Eve is now alienated from God and suffers death as a consequence. Of that, nobody was in any doubt. The question was whether human beings descended from Adam inherited his sin and the guilt attached to it. Here there was genuine hesitation. Some said that we do—everyone is guilty before God and in need of salvation for that reason. Others said that guilt can be applied only to particular individuals. I might suffer the consequences of Adam's sin, but I am not personally guilty because of it.

This became, and has remained, a point of difference between Western (Latin) Christianity, which generally follows Augustine of Hippo in regarding everyone as guilty, and the Eastern churches, which do not. It can be argued that the practical results are much the same—nobody goes to heaven apart from the saving grace of Christ—but it is fair to say that Western Christianity has traditionally paid much more attention to the atoning work of Christ and its significance than the Eastern churches have. All Christians regard the cross as the symbol of suffering and death for the sin of the world, but the Western churches have emphasized—and debated—the meaning and extent of Christ's sacrifice as a propitiation for sin and expiation of guilt in a way that is not so true of the East. Where do the church fathers stand on this?

There is little doubt that they all believed that the death to which Paul referred in Romans is spiritual. Origen said, "The death which entered through sin is without doubt that death of which the prophet speaks when he says: 'The soul which sins shall surely die.'[71] One might rightly say that our bodily death is a shadow of that death. For whenever a soul dies, the body has to follow suit."[72] That this spiritual death was the result of Adam's sin was universally acknowledged. In the same passage of his commentary, Origen answered those who were inclined to blame Eve, rather than Adam, by pointing out that the inheritance of sin (as of everything else) passed through the male line, the implication being that if Adam had not followed Eve, sin would not have had any consequences for their descendants. As it is, the sin of Adam has led to universal death, even for those who have not sinned in the way that he did.[73] Here we can observe a certain tension in the fathers. Pelagius (early fifth century), whom Augustine attacked as a heretic but who was highly regarded in much of the Christian world of his time, believed that there were some righteous people, like Abraham and Isaac, who did not sin as Adam did and so did not deserve to die, although they clearly did. The only explanation he could offer for that was that such people were so few in number that exceptions to the general rule could not be made. This seems unfair, but Pelagius could point out that even the righteous have to live an earthly, and not a heavenly, life, and as a result they have to suffer the consequences.[74]

The apparent injustice inherent in the belief that Adam's descendants suffer for sins they have not committed was addressed by Theodoret of Cyrrhus, who said that although everyone dies, each individual is punished for their own sins and not for that of Adam.[75]

---

71. Ezek 18:4.

72. Origen, *Commentary on Romans* 3.50.

73. John Chrysostom, *Homilies on Romans* 10.

74. Pelagius, *Commentary on Romans*, on Rom 5:12.

75. Theodoret of Cyrrhus, *Interpretation of the Letter to the Romans*, on Rom 5:12.

The weakness of that argument was that it was hard to see how it could be applied to children, particularly to infants who died before they had any opportunity to sin. Gennadius of Constantinople tackled that problem by saying that some die because of their own sins, while others die only because of Adam's condemnation, and he specifically mentioned children among the latter.[76] The issue was not finally settled until Oecumenius of Tricca (Trikkala), whose commentary probably dates from the sixth century. He said simply, "Adam is the origin and the cause of the fact that we have all sinned in imitation of him."[77] Oecumenius made no mention of any exceptions to the rule, so we must assume that he included infants among those who died because of Adam's sin, even if it was hard to see why they should.

Theodoret, Gennadius, and Oecumenius were all Greek writers from the Eastern church, and they reflect the difficulties and ambiguities of their tradition. In the Latin West a different atmosphere prevailed. Even before Augustine we find the main elements of his doctrine of sin already in evidence. Ambrose of Milan, for example, while paying due regard to the question of universal death, nevertheless proclaimed, "In Adam I fell, in Adam I was cast out of paradise, in Adam I died. How shall God call me back, except he find me in Adam? For just as in Adam I am guilty of sin and owe a debt to death, so in Christ I am justified."[78] Here the cosmic tragedy becomes intensely personal, as befits what was, after all, a funeral address.

Ambrose's contemporary Ambrosiaster agreed that all human beings sin because of their descent from Adam, but he has a curious take on the fate of souls after death: "Death is the separation

---

76. Gennadius of Constantinople, *Pauline Commentary from the Greek Church*, See Gerald Bray, ed., *Romans*, ACCS 6 (Downers Grove, IL: InterVarsity Press, 1998), on Rom 5:12.

77. Oecumenius of Tricca, *Pauline Commentary from the Greek Church*, See Gerald Bray, ed., *Romans*, ACCS 6 (Downers Grove, IL: InterVarsity Press, 1998), on Rom 5:12.

78. Ambrose of Milan, *On the Death of His Brother Satyrus* 2.6.

of body and soul. There is another death as well, called the second death, which takes place in Gehenna. We do not suffer this death as a result of Adam's sin, but his fall makes it possible for us to get it by our own sins. Good men were protected from this, as they were only in hell, but they were still not free, because they could not ascend to heaven. They were still bound by the sentence meted out in Adam, the seal of which was broken by the death of Christ."[79] The idea of the second death probably reflects Revelation 20:14–15, but the gradation of the underworld into hell and Gehenna may be original to Ambrosiaster. If so, it represents the first intimation of what would later be classified as the *limbus patrum*, or limbo, the place where unbaptized souls of those who have not committed actual sin go when they die. Ambrosiaster believed that these people would eventually be released, though he did not specify when that would occur. Once again, this would appear to be an early foreshadowing of the later belief in the so-called harrowing of hell, loosely based on 1 Peter 3:19, when Jesus descended there to proclaim the good news of salvation and release all those who were trapped through no fault of their own.

It was Augustine of course who examined this question most carefully and who came up with what would become the definitive Western position on the subject for the next thousand years. Augustine made it very clear that even little children have broken God's covenant, not because of any sin that they have committed, but because of our common descent from Adam.[80] By the same token, there was no degree of sinfulness involved in the condemnation of

---

79. Ambrosiaster, *Commentary on Paul's Epistles*, on Rom 5:12.
80. Augustine of Hippo, *City of God* 16.27; *Letters* 157.

the entire human race. Some people obviously sin more than others, but the basic fact of our condemnation is the same in every case.[81]

Here we are moving from a concept of sin as acts committed by individuals to one of sinfulness, a condition of alienation from God that extends to every human being. This may seem unfair in purely human terms, since most people think that the punishment ought to fit the crime, but that would open the door to gradations of sinners and allow human pride to claim greater righteousness for those who lived a moral life. Augustine's view stresses the complete equality of the human race in the presence of God and the equal applicability of Christ's redeeming sacrifice to all sorts and conditions of human beings. At the most basic level, all have sinned and come short of the glory of God, and it is only in and through the work of Christ that we can be restored to what he wants us to be.

The profundity of Augustine's analysis has never been surpassed, despite many attempts to deny its validity. Universal sinfulness is not a popular idea, and most of us like to think that some are better than others, even to the point of believing that they deserve to go to heaven because they are such "good" people. This is the very antithesis of the gospel, by which we are saved by grace through faith and not of ourselves, and Augustine's clear vision of that has remained foundational for the life and renewal of the church through the ages. His opinions can be refined and developed, as they have been over time, but they cannot be brushed aside as of no consequence. His teaching remains as important for us today as it has ever been and may rightly be seen as the crowning glory of the patristic era.

81. Augustine of Hippo, *Against Julian* 20.63.

HEBREWS 11:1–3

> Now faith is the assurance of things hoped for, the conviction
> of things not seen. For by it the people of old received their
> commendation. By faith we understand that the universe was
> created by the word of God, so that what is seen was not made
> out of things that are visible.

It is a commonplace of Christian theology that we are justified in
the sight of God by our faith. Disputes have arisen over the precise
relationship between faith and so-called works, but it is generally
agreed that what we do is a reflection of who we are and of what we
believe. Without faith, our actions, however noble and praiseworthy
they may be in themselves, have no context in which they might be
evaluated and therefore can have no saving power. Everything we
do finds its meaning and its justification in the relationship that we
have with God, and that relationship is defined by our faith in him.

But what exactly is faith? The anonymous writer to the Hebrews
addresses this question in his great letter, which is more properly
described as a sermon, and he illustrates his point with a catalog of
examples taken from the Old Testament. Faith is essentially trust
in the promises of God, revealed to us in the prophecies of ancient
Israel and largely fulfilled in the coming of Christ, though there is
yet more to come. Christians look to the examples of the past for
encouragement to persevere in the present, knowing that the God
who has brought us this far will see us through. As Theodoret of
Cyrrhus expressed it, every generation faces its own struggles, but
in the end we belong together and will receive the same heavenly
reward for our faithfulness.[82] Theodore of Mopsuestia pointed out

---

82. Theodoret of Cyrrhus, *Interpretation of Hebrews*, on Heb 11:1–2.

that Jewish reliance on keeping the law was in fact an admission of unbelief, since the Jews were afraid that if they did not do so, God would not bless them or protect them. But as Hebrews points out, even those who gave the law and who lived under it were men and women of faith above all else, because they were looking forward to the fulfillment of God's promises and not relying on their own efforts to earn credit with God.[83]

Why God should have delayed sending his Son into the world was a question that some of the early Christians asked, and Leo the Great provided an answer for them. He claimed that delaying salvation was a calculated move on God's part. The justification for that was that people were expected to grow in their faith as they waited for the promises to be fulfilled, and that by doing so, they would appreciate them all the more when that happened.[84] Leo was not really speaking about the ancient Israelites, who were not his immediate concern, but about the people of his own time, who had to learn the same patience in their own experience. This practical, pastoral aspect of living by faith was always at the forefront of the fathers' minds. Cyril of Jerusalem drew on everyday examples to demonstrate how important faith is in our lives: "By faith, the laws of marriage tie together people who have lived as strangers. ... By faith, farmers are encouraged, because someone who does not believe that the harvest will come will not endure such backbreaking work. By faith, sailors exchange solid ground for the tossing waves, committing themselves to uncertainty and carrying with them a faith that is stronger than any anchor. By faith, most human affairs are held together."[85]

83. Theodore of Mopsuestia, *Fragments on the Epistle to the Hebrews*, on Heb 11:1–2.

84. Leo the Great, *Sermons* 69.2.

85. Cyril of Jerusalem, *Catechetical Lectures* 5.3.

Given that reality, what difficulty could there be in believing that God, who has made the entire world, will not fulfill the promises he has given to his people? To refuse to believe in them until they have materialized is not faith, but lack of it, because nobody is challenged to believe in what they can see already.[86] The fathers understood that the primary purpose of faith was not to achieve material results but to deepen our relationship with God. Human minds believe in a chain of cause and effect, according to which what happens can be understood, and even predicted, by what already exists. But faith in God demands that we go one step further than this. We certainly believe that there are scientific laws in the universe that take effect according to predetermined patterns, but where do those laws come from? Who established them and how are they maintained? This can only be known by faith. As John Chrysostom observed, nobody except God was present to observe the creation of the universe, but it must have come from somewhere. It is far easier to believe that an all-knowing and all-powerful God made it than to surmise that it appeared of its own volition, since where would that volition have come from?[87]

Faith is demanding in some respects, but it is not irrational. On the contrary, it is the necessary starting point for life of any kind. If we had no hope for the future and no idea that anything that does not already exist might appear, what would be the point of living? As Augustine put it, "Faith does not falter because it is supported by hope. Take away hope and faith disappears. If you are walking somewhere, why would you ever move your feet if you have no hope of arriving at your destination? Furthermore, if you have no

---

86. Augustine of Hippo, *Sermons* 126.3.

87. John Chrysostom, *On the Epistle to the Hebrews* 22.1–2.

love, faith and hope are useless. Why bother hoping for something that you do not want?"[88]

Augustine went on to add that when our hope of attaining or achieving something is realized, faith disappears because it is no longer necessary. The message here is that faith lies at the heart of the Christian life because it is the substance or basis of the hope that the gospel gives us for the future. That hope in turn motivates us to act, so that we can enjoy and appreciate that future when it arrives. As long as we live in this world, we shall have goals toward which we strive, and no goal can be higher than the desire to live with God in eternity. The witness of past generations is presented to us for our encouragement and for our instruction. We are where we are now because of the faithfulness of our ancestors who built for a future that they themselves did not see. But they built, knowing that God would redeem the time and produce the results that we see today. We are called to walk in their footsteps and build for the future, not knowing when our labor will be rewarded, but sure that some day it will be.

This is the blueprint for the Christian life. Modern believers are called to walk in faith just as much as earlier generations were, expecting the same rewards to be revealed in God's good time. The fathers of the church could not know that we would still be reading their works today, nor could they have had any idea of how the gospel would spread across the world and take root in places of which they had never heard. Their faith has been vindicated in ways that they could not have known or suspected. We are called to learn from their example and to take heart in the fact that God has not changed, that his promises remain firm, and that in his good time he will reveal the fruits of our faith in the life of his people.

---

88. Augustine of Hippo, *Sermons* 359A.3–4.

REVELATION 20:1–6

Then I saw an angel coming down from heaven, holding in his
hand the key to the bottomless pit and a great chain. And he
seized the dragon, the ancient serpent, who is the devil and
Satan, and bound him for a thousand years, and threw him
into the pit, and shut it and sealed it over him, so that he might
not deceive the nations any longer, until the thousand years
were ended. After that he must be released for a little while.
Then I saw thrones, and seated on them were those to
whom the authority to judge was committed. Also I saw the
souls of those who had been beheaded for the testimony of
Jesus and for the word of God, and those who had not worshiped the beast or its image and had not received its mark on
their foreheads or their hands. They came to life and reigned
with Christ for a thousand years. The rest of the dead did not
come to life until the thousand years were ended. This is the
first resurrection. Blessed and holy is the one who shares in
the first resurrection! Over such the second death has no
power, but they will be priests of God and of Christ, and they
will reign with him for a thousand years.

The book of Revelation has always had a mysterious quality about
it, and the church fathers were well aware of that. Modern scholars
have come to recognize a genre of apocalyptic literature, of which
they have found numerous examples, but although the canonical
book of Revelation is counted among them, it stands out as unique.
Other apocalypses are attributed to figures from the distant and
semi-mythical past, such as Enoch, but the New Testament text
was written by John, who claimed to have had the vision himself.
Whether this John was the disciple of Jesus, who wrote the Fourth
Gospel and at least 1 John, if not 2 and 3 John as well, was debated

in ancient times, much as it is now, with opinions divided.[89] In the Greek church there were some who doubted Revelation's canonicity, and it was not until the sixth century or even later that it was fully accepted as Scripture. The Western church was more accommodating, but even there, commentaries on the book did not appear until the very end of the patristic period. On the other hand, many of the elements contained in it were frequently discussed, not least the defeat of Satan and the thousand-year reign of the saints. To a church that had endured persecution for two and a half centuries, the imagery of spiritual warfare that the book describes was very real, and identifications with contemporary politics came naturally to many.

At a deeper theological level, Revelation raised the question of eschatology, which is inherent in the Christian message. Christ will come again at the end of time to judge the living and the dead, but how will that happen? We are warned not to guess the future—he will come as a thief in the night, when he is least expected—but we must be constantly on our guard so that when that moment arrives we shall not be found wanting (1 Thess 5:2; 2 Pet 3:10). How the events described in Revelation should be interpreted became a major question, particularly as the Roman Empire collapsed and the end of time seemed to many to be imminent.

Augustine of Hippo spoke directly to the question of the thousand-year reign of the saints and argued that it could be interpreted in one of two ways: "One interpretation is that this will all happen in the sixth and last millennium [after the creation], which is now passing, and that when John spoke of the 'thousand years' he was using the whole figuratively, to represent only a part of it. ... The

---

89. Dionysius of Alexandria (c. 247–265) dismissed it completely, according to Eusebius of Caesarea, who recorded his adverse judgment (*Ecclesiastical History* 7.25.22).

other interpretation makes the 'thousand years' stand for the entire Christian era, a perfect number being used to indicate the fullness of time."[90] The first of these interpretations may be regarded as more literal than the second, but in fact both are symbolic. Oecumenius noted that the psalmist had said that in God's eyes a thousand years was like a single day, or a watch in the night (Ps 90:4), and so it could not be calculated in the normal way. He himself preferred the view that it equated to the time of Christ's incarnation, when the devil was supposedly bound.[91] Like many others, he linked this to the words of Jesus about the need to "bind the strong man" before robbing him (Matt 12:29; Mark 3:27). The fathers readily identified the strong man with Satan, and binding him was the necessary prelude to setting his captives free, which is what the Son of God had come to earth to do.[92]

There were, however, a number of interpreters who treated the thousand years as literal and even set precise bounds to them. Andrew of Caesarea, for example, said that they represented the time from the incarnation of Christ to the coming of the antichrist, whereas Caesarius of Arles counted them from the crucifixion.[93] These differences are reminiscent of the divergent calculations that some overenthusiastic Christians still make today, though there is an important difference. Modern speculators usually put the date of Christ's return in the relatively near future, and so the failure of their predictions to materialize is soon spotted. But the fathers had no such worries. Even on the most generous estimates, there would

---

90. Augustine of Hippo, *City of God* 20.7.

91. Oecumenius, *Commentary on the Apocalypse* 20.1–3.

92. This was also stated by Primasius, *Commentary on the Apocalypse* 20.2, and by Augustine of Hippo in the passage just quoted.

93. Andrew of Caesarea, *Explanation of the Apocalypse* 20.2; Caesarius of Arles, *Exposition of the Apocalypse* 20.3; *Homily* 17.

still be at least five centuries before Christ would return, and so they had little reason to fear that their prophecies would be disproved in their own lifetimes.

Revelation 20:3 says that at the end of the thousand years the devil will be released for a little while—three and a half years, to be exact. The shortness of the time was a comfort in some respects, but it still required explanation. Augustine was not worried, because he believed that the devil would be making war only on people who would be beyond his ability to overpower. He argued, though, that Satan had to be set free: "If he were never set free, the full measure of his malevolent power would never be known, nor would the full measure of the holy city's staunchness under fire be put to the test."[94]

Augustine placed these events in a distant and undefined future, but Oecumenius thought that the three and a half years symbolically represented the time from Christ's incarnation until his return—now, in other words. This encouraged him to think that the return of the Lord must be imminent, since the symbolic time was so short.[95] Augustine preferred to identify the thousand-year reign of the saints (and the concurrent binding of Satan) with the present age between the first and second coming of Christ, which he saw as a foretaste of the final and eternal reign that would follow the loosing and eventual destruction of the devil. The thousand-year reign was therefore not the final triumph but a period in which the church will continue to do battle with its spiritual enemies.[96]

As for the first resurrection and the second death, the general consensus of the fathers was that the first referred to the resurrection of believers at the second coming of Christ. They would be

---

94. Augustine of Hippo, *City of God* 20.8.

95. Oecumenius, *Commentary on the Apocalypse* 20.1–3.

96. Augustine of Hippo, *City of God* 20.9.

protected by their faith from the consequences of the final judgment, which would follow on that resurrection, but unbelievers would be condemned to a second, spiritual death, which would be eternal. Victorinus of Pettau ventured to suggest that the 144,000 mentioned in Revelation 14:1–5 would be the number of Jews who would be converted during this time, though he seems to have been the only one to voice such an opinion.[97]

It is difficult for modern readers to know what to make of these patristic speculations. They both amuse and perplex us in varying degrees, though with the advantage of several centuries of hindsight we can at least rule out some of their more precise conclusions. Christ did not return in the year 1000, however we might calculate that, and we must be wary of attempts to put times and dates on the events Revelation describes. At the same time, we must also recognize that speculation about these things is far from dead, and that the years around 2000 saw a small revival of interest in the millennium. The whole subject remains a mystery, and we should not pride ourselves on being any wiser than the church fathers were. They were guessing at what they could not know, and if we are honest, we cannot do much better than they did. The return of Christ remains as much a matter of faith for us as it was for them, and only when it happens will we fully know what the meaning of the Apocalypse really is.

---

97. Victorinus of Pettau, *Commentary on the Apocalypse* 20.1–2.

# VI

## SEVEN THESES ON HOW THE CHURCH FATHERS READ THE BIBLE

In concluding our study of the biblical interpretation of the church fathers, the following points should be borne in mind. The fathers were not perfect, and not everything they had to say has stood the test of time, but on certain fundamental principles they remain authoritative guides for the church today. The following are of special importance:

1. The Bible contains the sum of Christian doctrine and is its only source.

2. The Bible is a revelation from God and the ultimate foundation of all knowable truth.

3. Jesus Christ is the theme of the Scriptures, which must be interpreted in the light of his life, death, and resurrection.

4. The substance of the biblical message is more important than its form.

5. The validity of a particular interpretation of the Bible must be tested against the text and not be determined by the standing or reputation of the interpreter.

6. The modern church must respect the fathers and be prepared to learn from them but without idolizing them or claiming for them an authority that they did not claim for themselves.

7. The Bible must be read and understood in the context of praise and worship.

## THE SEVEN THESES

### I. THE BIBLE CONTAINS THE SUM OF CHRISTIAN DOCTRINE AND IS ITS ONLY SOURCE.

This belief undergirds the whole of the early church's interpretation of the Bible. Writers like Origen and Augustine believed in a systematic approach to theology, which for them meant developing a consistent hermeneutic of the Scriptures. They believed that the text revealed the mind of God, who is both the Creator and the Redeemer of the world. The basic message of the Bible is clear and easy to understand, though many individual passages are obscure to the untrained reader. It is the task of the interpreter to begin with the basic principles, which the patristic tradition formulated in the Apostles' and Nicene Creeds, and move from them to a deeper understanding of the spiritual truths which they contain. No belief that is not found in the Bible, or that is not compatible with it, can be accepted as Christian teaching. Nor is it right to start with a philosophical framework and make the biblical texts conform to it because the Bible is its own philosophy, grounded in divine revelation and not based on human reason.

## 2. THE BIBLE IS A REVELATION FROM GOD AND THE ULTIMATE FOUNDATION OF ALL KNOWABLE TRUTH.

The worldview revealed in the Bible is the foundation of all truth. This is particularly important when it comes to the doctrines of creation, and of the nature of good and evil. Everything that exists has been made by God for a purpose, even if that purpose is known only to him. God loves everything that he has made and sees it as good in itself. That does not mean that there is no potential for development within the created order, because God gave human beings the power to exploit the resources that he provided for them, but it does mean that nothing in creation can be rejected on the ground that it is evil or unclean. Sin and evil do not inhere in things but are expressions of rebellion against God, of which all human beings are guilty.

It is possible for sinful human beings to have some knowledge of God and of his creation because we have all been created in his image, but whatever knowledge we have is obscured by our separation from him. Only a person filled with the Holy Spirit and guided by him can understand why God has made the world in the way that he has and be guided to the right use of the created order.

## 3. JESUS CHRIST IS THE THEME OF THE SCRIPTURES, WHICH MUST BE INTERPRETED IN THE LIGHT OF HIS LIFE, DEATH, AND RESURRECTION.

Many centuries before the coming of Jesus Christ into the world, God revealed himself to prophets and leaders whom he used to form a nation that would be set apart for him and prepared to receive the coming of the Savior in due course. The first person to receive this revelation was Abraham, and the nation to which he gave birth was Israel, whose history is recounted in the Hebrew Scriptures, or (in Christian terms) the Old Testament. This revelation is authentic and provides the information we need to interpret the life of Jesus Christ correctly.

The coming of Christ into the world has fulfilled many of the promises and prophecies found in the Old Testament, but its spiritual message has been validated by his life, death, and resurrection. It has not been superseded, and Christians continue to study the ancient Hebrew oracles because they see the person and work of Christ revealed in them. Every part of the biblical text has some relation to Christ, though this may not be immediately apparent on the surface. In those cases, the skill of gifted interpreters is required to make it clear how the message of Christ is proclaimed in them. This may require transcending the literal sense of the text, but that is justified if it brings us closer to understanding who Jesus is and what he has done for us.

### 4. THE SUBSTANCE OF THE BIBLICAL MESSAGE IS MORE IMPORTANT THAN ITS FORM.

The message of the text is what counts, and it can be expressed in many different ways. Translations of the original documents are possible and have been used by God, even if they have not always captured the precise meaning of the original. This is because the mind of God is not confined to only one language or form. This helps to explain why the church fathers saw little need to learn Hebrew in order to understand the Old Testament, and even the Latin-speakers did not find it necessary to master Greek in order to understand the New. They believed that if the message is true it can be conveyed in any language, because although God accommodates himself to human speech, he is not limited by it. He makes his meaning clear to the spiritually minded, who are the only people capable of understanding what he is really saying. Today we pay more attention to the original languages than the fathers did, but their belief that the message can be conveyed in any language is one that we still accept. Very few people today can read the original texts, but the work of translation continues apace, and millions of people can testify that God speaks to them just as clearly as he spoke to those to whom the revelation was first given.

## 5. THE VALIDITY OF A PARTICULAR INTERPRETATION OF THE BIBLE MUST BE TESTED AGAINST THE TEXT AND NOT BE DETERMINED BY THE STANDING OR REPUTATION OF THE INTERPRETER.

Many great biblical interpreters had troubled relationships with the church. Pelagius, for example, was accused of heresy, but his commentaries were so valuable that they were saved and recycled under other names. Tyconius was a schismatic, but his theories were good enough to be adopted by Augustine, who felt perfectly free to acknowledge his source. Origen was condemned three centuries after his death, and his interpretations of Scripture were largely discounted, but by then his influence had spread so far and gone so deep that it could not be eradicated. The fathers were happy to preserve what they found valuable in his legacy and ignored the rest. Over time, a consensus emerged that was not dependent on the reputation of any one individual. The fathers retained the respect of later generations, who acknowledged their authority, but they did not claim infallibility.

When controversies arose about the right way to interpret the biblical revelation, the matters in question were debated and decided, sometimes after decades of argument, by councils of the church that strove to find a common mind. The followers of Arius used

biblical texts to support their view that Jesus Christ was not God in
the same absolute sense that the Father was, but their opinion was
refuted by others who went beyond the superficial statements of
the biblical text to examine their logical implications. In the same
way, the doctrine of the Trinity was expounded by examining the
witness of the Scriptures as a whole and not relying exclusively on
one or two passages taken out of context. In this, as in other similar
instances, the fathers adopted a method of interpretation that has
stood the test of time, even when their interpretations of particular
words and verses have been challenged and sometimes discarded
by subsequent commentators.

6. THE MODERN CHURCH MUST RESPECT THE
FATHERS AND BE PREPARED TO LEARN FROM
THEM, BUT WITHOUT IDOLIZING THEM OR
CLAIMING FOR THEM AN AUTHORITY THAT
THEY DID NOT CLAIM FOR THEMSELVES.

The church fathers wanted to be faithful to the teaching of holy
Scripture, which they regarded as the word of God. In that respect,
Christians today are one with them, and we must listen to them as
we would listen to fellow believers, whoever they are. But we must
also remember that they labored under great difficulties. They did
not have ready access to the Hebrew Old Testament and were not
always able to check the accuracy of their manuscripts. On the other
hand, they had direct experience of the ancient world and a feel for
the oral culture out of which the written texts emerged. They were
not naively literalistic in their interpretations, nor were they gullible
or easily fooled. They had been converted to a biblical worldview
that was completely different from the culture into which they had
been born, and they understood the significance of that better than
many modern people do. Like all human beings, they made mistakes

and they can be faulted on points of detail, but their fundamental outlook was sound. They are indeed our fathers in the faith, and we must honor them as such, even as we go beyond them, using tools and techniques of analysis that were unknown to them. If we can sometimes reach further than they could, it is because we stand on the shoulders of giants, and their legacy is one for which we must be forever grateful. We build on the foundations that have been laid for us, just as the fathers themselves did, and as generations yet unborn will continue to do until Christ comes again (Eph 2:19–22).

## 7. THE BIBLE MUST BE READ AND UNDERSTOOD IN THE CONTEXT OF PRAISE AND WORSHIP.

The fathers read and expounded the Scriptures in public worship. Many of the sources we use to understand what they taught come to us in the form of sermons. It does not matter whether those sermons represent the actual words they used—probably many of them were edited for publication or transcribed from notes taken by others who heard them preach. The important point is that the exposition was set in the context of worship. The Psalter was in constant use as the hymn book of the early church, and the ancient liturgies that have come down to us are suffused with biblical quotations which have bene turned into congregational prayer and praise. It was the conviction of the fathers that only those whose hearts and minds were attuned to the worship of God would hear him speaking to them and be transformed by the inner work of his Holy Spirit in their lives. Centuries of study and scholarship have done nothing to alter this understanding, and Christians today are at one with the fathers as we stand around the throne of grace, hearing God speak to us in his word and being changed by it as his timeless message does its work in us.

# GENERAL INDEX

## A

Abraham 59, 72, 91, 168, 184

Adam and Eve 59, 77, 81, 124, 128, 137–39, 164, 166–71

Alaric 80

Alexandria 15, 18, 38–41

allegory 60, 74, 91, 115–16, 124, 139, 148–49

Ambrose of Milan 30, 40–42, 123, 149–50, 154–55, 169

Ambrosiaster 30, 41, 122, 169–70

Andrew of Caesarea 116–17, 178

Antioch 38–41

Antiochus IV Epiphanes 53

Apocrypha 19–21, 131, 135

Apollinarius 39

Apostles' Creed 2, 143, 182

Aquila 5, 18

Arianism, Arius 29, 39, 185–86

Aramaic language 4, 9n, 23

Armenian language 24

Athanasian Creed 2

Athanasius 28, 39, 145

Athens 65, 82–83

Augustine of Hippo 4n, 19–20, 23, 28–31, 41, 43, 47–48, 50, 69,
80–81, 118–27, 129–30, 133, 138, 142–43, 145, 150, 164, 166–67, 169–71, 174, 177–79, 185

## B

Babylon 81, 120

Baruch 13

Basil of Caesarea 40, 110–11, 113

Beatus of Liébana 120

Bede 3, 42, 50, 131, 155

Beza, Theodore 27

Buddeus, Johann Franz 1–2

## C

Caesarea Maritima 18, 38

Caesarius of Arles 178

Calvin, John 93

Cassiodorus 30, 130–31

Chalcedon, Council of 2, 39–42, 146–47

Chromatius 159

Claudius (Emperor) 54

Clement of Alexandria 37, 47, 89–92, 137

Codex, codices 26

Constantine I 39

189

Constantinople 39
Constantinople, First Council of 2
Constantinople, Second Council of 74
Coptic language 24
creation 68–76, 136–40
Cyprian of Carthage 28
Cyril of Alexandria 39–40, 115–16, 130, 146
Cyril of Jerusalem 173

D
Damasus I, Pope 25
David 13, 75, 144–47
Diadochus of Photice 138
Didymus the Blind 39, 69
Diodore of Tarsus 111, 115
Donatism 31, 119

E
Elijah 12, 143, 157–59
Elisha 12
Ephesus, First Council of 2
Ephraim (Ephrem) the Syrian 42, 69
Epicureans 78
Erasmus, Desiderius 4, 30
Eucherius of Lyon 130
Eusebius of Caesarea 109–10, 145–47
Eustathius of Antioch 109

G
Gennadius of Constantinople 168–69
Gerhard, Johannes 1–2
Gnosticism 33–35, 67, 91
God-fearers 55
Greek language 4, 9, 23–25, 33, 42, 121, 153, 184
Gregory of Nazianzus 40, 145–46, 163
Gregory of Nyssa 40, 113–14, 138

Gregory I the Great, Pope 42, 161

H
Harnack, Adolf von 82
Hebrew language 4, 9, 14–15, 137, 153, 184
Hermas, Shepherd of 26
Hezekiah 152
Hilary of Poitiers 158–59, 165
Homer 23, 90

I
Irenaeus 28, 35, 128, 137
Isaiah 13, 152–56
Islam 82

J
Jeremiah 13
Jerome 2, 4, 18, 20, 25, 28, 30–31, 37, 42, 50, 69, 109, 119–21, 130, 155, 160
Jesus Christ 10–13, 27–28, 53, 56, 59–60, 64, 67, 72, 77, 79–80, 89, 108, 116, 122, 137, 143–47, 150, 152–53, 156–66
Jews, Judaism 53–61
John (Apostle) 33, 176
John the Baptist 157
John Cassian 104, 106
John Chrysostom 4n, 30, 39, 43, 48–49, 61, 69, 139, 153, 158–59, 161, 164, 166, 174
John of Damascus 3
Josephus, Flavius 13
Justin Martyr 34, 57–64, 89, 142, 154, 163
Justinian I 82

**K**

Kannengiesser, Charles 6–7, 32n

**L**

Lateran Council, Fourth 3
Latin language 4, 25, 39–42, 109,
    117–18, 120, 184
Leo I the Great, Pope 145
Luther, Martin 3–4, 84

**M**

Marcion 22, 36, 118
Marcus Aurelius 79
Marius Victorinus 137
Mary, Virgin 59, 116
Masoretes 14–15
matrimony 72–74
Maximus of Turin 160
Melchizedek 59
Migne, Jacques-Paul 2
Mishnah 56
Monophysitism 40, 42
monotheism 65–67
Montanism 31, 35–36, 80, 118
Moses 12, 59, 63, 90, 109, 143, 157–59

**N**

Neoplatonism 82
Nestorius, Nestorianism 39–40, 42
Nicene Creed 182
Nilus of Ancyra 149–51
Noah 100–103, 106
Novatian 155
Nicaea, First Council of 2, 39

**O**

Octateuch 131

Oecumenius of Tricca 116–17, 169, 177,
    179
Origen 18, 28n, 30, 37–41, 47–48,
    69, 92–103, 105–7, 109–11,
    113, 120–21, 130–32, 138–39,
    141–42, 158, 160, 167, 185

**P**

Papias 22
Paul (Apostle) 3, 11–12, 19–21, 23–24,
    33, 36, 54, 70, 72, 83–84, 89,
    94, 97, 137, 157
Pelagius 30–31, 41, 43, 127, 168, 185
Peter (Apostle) 22–24, 33
Peter Chrysologus 159
Philo of Alexandria 89–91
Plato, Platonism 23, 63, 82–83, 87, 89
Plotinus 82
Pontius Pilate 54
Porphyry 82–83
Primasius of Hadrumetum 120
Proclus 82
Procopius of Gaza 40, 131
Prosper of Aquitaine 130
Psalms, Psalter 17, 144–47, 187
Ptolemy II 15

**R**

Rome 39, 80, 117
Rufinus of Aquileia 37, 120

**S**

Saint Maur, monks of 2
Samaritans 12, 16
Samuel 140–44
Satan 77–78, 157–62, 179
Saul (king) 140–44

Septuagint 4, 8n, 16, 18–19, 29, 50, 118, 149
Socrates 62, 84
Solomon 74–75
Song of Songs (Solomon) 73–74, 94–95, 98, 126, 148–52
Stoics 78
Symmachus 5
Syriac language 24, 42

**T**
Talmud 56
Tarphon (Trypho) 34, 57–58
Tatian 22
Tertullian of Carthage 31, 35–36, 46, 66, 80, 83, 118, 142, 165
theodicy 76–79

Theodore of Mopsuestia 39, 41, 74, 111–113, 115, 164–65, 172
Theodoret of Cyrrhus 39, 114–15, 147, 150, 168–69, 172
Theodotion 5, 18
Theophilus of Antioch 66
Theophylact of Ochrid 153
Tyconius 31, 41, 43, 47, 119, 125–29, 133, 185
typology 60

**V**
Victorinus of Pettau 119–20, 179
Vulgate Bible (Latin) 4, 25

**Z**
Zion 81, 104, 110

# SCRIPTURE INDEX

## Old Testament

### Genesis

1:26–27 ............... 136–40
3................................... 60
27:27–29 ..................... 115

### Exodus

15:27........................... 114
17:11 ........................... 115

### Deuteronomy

6:13............................. 157
6:6............................... 157
8:3............................... 156

### 1 Samuel

28:1–25 ...................... 109
28:13–14 ............. 140–44

### Psalms

19 ................................ 68
19:7 ............................. 84
22:1–8 ................. 144–47
23................................. 17
90:4 ........................... 177
91:11 ........................... 157
91:12 ........................... 157
137 ............................. 120

### Proverbs

8:22............................. 29

### Song of Songs

2:1–4 ..................... 148–52
2:4................................ 74

### Isaiah

7:14 ...................... 152–56
9:6 ........................ 152–56
19:1 ............................ 110
28:14–17 ..................... 110

## New Testament

### Matthew

4:1–11 ................. 156–162
12:29 .......................... 178
12:38–42 ..................... 111
16:18 ........................... 24
24:37–39 ..................... 101

### Mark

3:27 ............................ 178

### Luke

4:16–21 ......................... 11
17:26–27 ..................... 101

### John

1:3................................ 29
3:3–8 .................. 162–166
4:24............................. 27
6:9............................... 116

## Acts

8:27–35 .......................... 10
14:11 ............................. 24
17:11 .............................. 11
17:23 ............................. 65

## Romans

5:12–14 ................. 166–171
7:12 .............................. 84

## 1 Corinthians

3:22 .............................. 23
6:3 ............................... 137
11:1 .............................. 112
12 ................................. 48
14 ................................. 48
15:28 ........................... 80

## 2 Corinthians

3:13 ............................. 109

## Galatians

1:18 .............................. 23
2:9–14 ........................... 23
4:6 ............................... 57

## Ephesians

2:19–22 ....................... 187

## 1 Thessalonians

5:2 .............................. 177

## 2 Timothy

3:16 .............................. 56

## Hebrews

1:1 .............................. 108
11:1–3 ................... 171–175
11:39–40 .................... 143

## 1 Peter

3:18–20 ...................... 101

## 2 Peter

1:21 .............................. 56
3:10 ............................. 177

## Revelation

7:3–4 ............................ 99
14:1–5 .......... 99–100, 179
20:1–6 ................. 175–179
21 ................................ 118

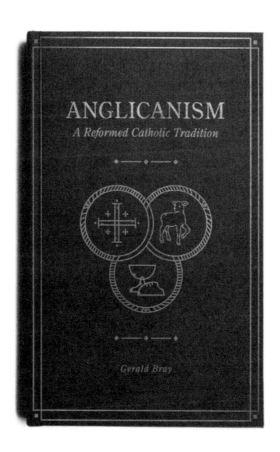

# ALSO AVAILABLE FROM GERALD BRAY

*Anglicanism: A Reformed Catholic Tradition*

---

**Visit lexhampress.com to learn more**